Beholding
&
Proclaiming
Reimagining the Art of Preaching
Reclaiming the Training of Preachers

Kristian Hernandez

Rev Ieisha Hawley

Kristian Hernandez

ISBN: 1720355398

ISBN-13: 978-1720355397

DEDICATION

I dedicate this book to the Lord Jesus Christ. I was a 14 year old kid when I first encountered his grace and love, and have never been the same since. All that I have in my life are undeserved gifts from his hand. May I always seek to live in gratitude for all you have done. I pray this book would glorify you and be used to raise up a new generation of preachers that would spread the fire of your love everywhere you send them.

Endorsements

"Kristian served as a leader in Resurrection church for over two decades. Among the many things he accomplished was developing a Preaching community as well as helping us develop our emerging young preachers. He is a great communicator who also knows how to equip other able ministers of the Word. Hence, this book is not mere theory but is a proven, practical tool for the Body of Christ!"
- Dr. Joseph Mattera
Overseeing Bishop of Christ Covenant Coalition and Resurrection Church of NY
New York, NY

"I wish I read this book when I first started out in ministry. Kristian Hernandez unpacks an approach to preaching (and training preachers) that is biblical, engaging, memorable, and practical. I am deeply appreciative of his work and I plan on referring this text to pastors and preachers for years to come."
- Drew Hyun
Founder, Hope Church NYC

New York, NY

"In the last 25 years of ministry I have seen many emerging leaders all of them incredibly talented, called of God, possessing God given ability and grace utilized to achieve and launch transformational movements in their local, regional and national assignments. However, I have yet to meet someone like Kristian Hernandez an unassuming called prophet to the City while simultaneously called to develop prophets in the Kingdom. It has been said that Charles Spurgeon was called the Prince of Preachers in his day, but perhaps his greatest Kingdom contribution was not his own preaching, but the scores of preachers he developed. It seems that Kristian is also graced with that royal blood to not only preach the "Kerygma", but is also called to develop others as they fine-tune their craft in preaching the "Kerygma". Kristian's manuscript and published work will prove to produce "Subject Matter Experts" among the Lay and Ordained among the Reformed and the Pentecostal! All who read and drink from the fount of Kristian's work will dive into a clear and succinct understanding of the power and relevance of the sacred art of preaching."
- Rev. Dr. Michael Carrion
National Director, National Latino Evangelical Coalition

"I've met a lot of great preachers over the years, but not many who can reproduce their gift. I have seen Kristian first hand develop preachers time and time again. This book expertly distills that wisdom in a way that will help pastors everywhere have a vision for and next steps to start training future preachers right away. A must read!"
- Justin Mattera
Lead Pastor, Zion
Brooklyn, NY

"Preaching books are many but preachers who are sharing their own journey as a preacher are few. Here is a honest transparent encouragement to all developing preachers who face many of the things shared in this book. Read and ponder."
- Dr. Frank Damazio
Lead Pastor, City Bible Church
Portland, OR

"The challenge of communicating the gospel in a clear, compassionate and convincing manner on a weekly basis to a broken and confused culture can be overwhelming. So when someone with the experience, wisdom and passion of Kristian Hernandez offers you a helping hand, you take it. In this unique guide to the preparation and practice of preaching, you'll find practical tools to sharpen and streamline your weekly process, resulting in an increasing ease and effectiveness in ministry. I recommend this timely resource to you."
- Dr. David Cannistraci
Lead Pastor, GateWay City Church
San Jose, CA

"Kristian Hernandez cares deeply about pastors, a fact which jumps off of every page of this excellent book. With wisdom alongside humility, Hernandez offers busy pastors a glimpse into his own life as a preacher, but also helpful tools for any pastor who wants to develop his or her preaching voice."
- Steve Wiens, Author of *Beginnings* (2016) and *Whole* (2017)

"In *Beholding & Proclaiming* Kristian gives us a peak into his preaching journey while laying out the need for multiplication in the Kingdom through the declarative word of God.
If there was ever a time for a book like this it is NOW!
I strongly urge you to read this book, digest it thoroughly and allow God to impregnate you with a fresh word for a new season."

- Rev. Adam Durso, Executive Director
LeadNYC.com

"Fewer people are reading the Bible and being transformed by it. Personal and corporate study of scripture has a diminishing rate of returns. Kris' book can and will change this trend. *Beholding and Proclaiming* provides a practical and helpful framework for engaging the Scriptures that opens the heart of the reader to the power of the gospel first, and then step by step create a meaningful sermon that leads to lasting impact. Behold first. Then proclaim. It's that simple. You won't regret reading this book."
- Guy Wasko
Lead Pastor, Trinity Grace East Village
New York, NY

"In *Beholding and Proclaiming* Kristian Hernandez introduces preachers to a surprisingly simple yet radically comprehensive approach to sermon preparation. In contrast to the helter-skelter manner many pastors go about their work, Kris shows how each step of sermon writing can be a God-oriented, prayer-saturated, Jesus-exalting, gospel-renewing, heart-transforming, mission-engaging walk with the Spirit. *Beholding and Proclaiming* is a refreshing book, not least because of its convicting power, that has the added bonus of serving as a manual for training preachers in your own congregation. I warmly commend it to you."
- Matthew Hoskinson, Ph.D.
Pastor, The First Baptist Church in the City of New York
New York, NY

"Kristian Hernandez has read most of the best preaching books circulating in the Christian world today. Like a great chef, he draws on the best ingredients from these books and mixes them together in *Beholding and Proclaiming*. The result is a brief, refreshing, and surprisingly comprehensive framework for preaching and raising up new preachers which is Spirit-anointed, Christ-centered, and exegetically sound. Kristian's humility, wisdom, and passion are compelling, as is the way he shares his own life story and faith journey throughout the book. I love developing new campus ministers as preachers. This is now my go-to text book."
- Greg Johnson, M.Div.
Divisional Ministry Director, InterVarsity South Coast New England

"At a time when "Do It Yourself" and "Quick-fixes" are overtaking the spiritual landscapes of our churches, we need a resource that will call us back to the things that are of utmost importance in ministry. We need a tool that allows us to refocus and re-center our preaching and teaching. Kristan Hernandez provides us with a fresh look at ministry and a challenge to return to the foundations that bring life to us and ultimately to our ministry. I recommend this book as a valuable resource for you whether you are just beginning or you have been serving the Lord for years!"
- Ralph T. Vogel
Lead Pastor, Church at the Heights
Gibsonia, PA

"In an era that is ever infatuated with the "new", Kristian Hernandez's *Beholding and Proclaiming* suggests that we need less new and more reminders of what is eternally true. This book artfully integrates ancient wisdom/ practices with modern realities to provide a framework for anyone interested in making disciples- and is particularly germane for those who feel called to communicate the Gospel. This book belongs in the toolkit of anyone interested in increasing the biblical literacy of those in their sphere of influence."
-John Kim
Lead Pastor, The 166 Vineyard Church
New York, NY

"I'm adding this book to the list of resources for church planters and multiplying churches! I can hand it confidently to anyone serious about their own preaching and a desire to multiply preachers. This is a resource that combines relational mentoring, personal transformation, in depth biblical study, and preaching praxis all in one. Kristian's matrix preaching model inspires us to develop and multiply the next generation of preachers who effectively proclaim the Gospel in their context."
-Gabe Barreiro
Supervisor, North Pacific District The Foursquare Church

"Kristian is tapping into a huge gap in our theological education and training. With all the hoops leaders go through to become more effective one of the most underserved areas is preaching. For many a theological education is unaffordable and if there is one area a pastor must be effective in to take their ministry to the next level its the area of preaching. In *Beholding and Proclaiming* Kristian gives practical steps that will guide pastors, laymen and any other Christian minister to a clear way to communicate a message from the Word of God. I recommend this for your church, your leaders but more so for your own effectiveness in telling the greatest story ever told…The Gospel!"
- James Roberson
Lead Pastor, Bridge Church
Brooklyn, NY

"I would like to meet the rare person who would not benefit from this labor of love from Kristian. He is humble, funny, and ultimately super accessible. And his dream to grow up more preachers for the sake of the gospel is made possible by the bottom-shelf practicality of this book. I could hear his voice as I read it. And if you haven't met him, you will through this book. And it will make you smile."
- Greg Gibbs, M.A.,
Lead Navigator, Auxano

"The ministry of preaching is one that consistently needs to be explored and reengaged in every generation. Moreover, the creation of a culture that trains and reproduces proclaimers of the gospel is indispensable to the future life of the church. I'm very grateful that Kristian Hernandez has a passion to see the Body of Christ equipped in these areas. This book is an important resource to establish a much needed culture in our local churches."
- Rich Villodas
Lead Pastor, New Life Fellowship Church
Queens, NY

"Kristian is an experienced, ever-growing, well respected Second-Gen Latino preacher ministering effectively in the multicultural complex mosaic of NYC. The primary passion that gives birth to this book - a sustainable pipeline of reproducing preachers within the pressing need for healthy, gospel renewing churches - as well as Kristian's clarion call to the church universal to prophetically proclaim contextual sermons that reflect the preacher's own journey and encounter with the living Christ as she/he

engages the text, leads me to wholeheartedly and enthusiastically
recommend reading Beholding and Proclaiming."
- Robert Guerrero
VP NYC, Redeemer City to City
New York, NY

"There's is always a temptation to develop as a preacher in the same way we
might develop as a salesman or CEO. Kristian offers a powerful challenge
in this book that brings us back to a simple reality that needs to be stated
over and over again: We preach and lead from who we are not just what we
know. He calls us to a lifestyle not just a set of skills and challenges
preachers to examine not just their doctrine but there life as well. This is a
valuable resource for anyone learning to preach or training others to
preach."
- Jay Pathak
Lead Pastor, The Mile High Vineyard and co-author of *The Art of
Neighboring*
Denver, CO

"With clarity and conviction, Kristian unpacks a preaching matrix that
transforms the art of preaching. As a gifted and passionate communicator,
Kristian takes the preacher on a journey from personal Gospel application
to sound and thorough handling of the Scriptures. His plea to slow down
and experience Christ in the text puts an end to selling a Gospel we haven't
yet savored ourselves. When applied, the practical tools Kristian offers will
shape and sharpen your sermons. I highly recommend this resource to
you."
- Justin Kendrick
Lead Pastor, City Church
New Haven, CT

"Let's face it: preachers are not born... they're made. Kristian Hernandez
offers an insightful, pragmatic, and honest reflection on the journey of
crafting a sermon, but more importantly invites gifted, called, and (perhaps)
un-initiated preachers to explore what it looks like to point others to Jesus
through their own journey of discovery and listening to God's Word."
- Glenn Peterson
Director of Church Planting, ECCC

"When Kristian first shared with me that he was working on this book, my
heart leapt. With an emphatic "YES!" I celebrated in advance a book that I
knew would be as inspiring as it would be practical. He is a craftsman,
sharing his craft. *Beholding and Proclaiming* re-energized my preaching and
challenged me in ways I needed challenge. I am thrilled to be able to

provide a much needed resource to leaders and preachers who are longing to not just be better communicators, but better agents of transformation in the lives of real people."
- Bradley W. Wiliams
Lead Pastor, Summit Church
New York City Coordinator, The Foursquare Church
Spokane, WA

"I met Kristian over ten years ago, at the Lausanne Conference for Younger Leaders in Malaysia. Since then, I have had the privilege of getting to know him not only as a pastor, but as a dear friend. He lives what he writes. His passion of preaching comes out of his deeper passion, beholding the glory of God in the Scriptures. I love how simple and practical the book is, and yet if you apply these principles, you will never stop unearthing new truths about Christ, and like those first apostles, you won't be able to hold it in. May this book be used to raise up a new generation of preachers who will spread a movement of gospel multiplication!"
- David Choi
Lead Pastor, Church of the Beloved
Chicago, IL

"I've been privileged to know Kristian for over 20 years, watching him grow from a young street preacher to a serious student to a pastor and relevant, compelling communicator. I've always been amazed at his rare ability to communicate the truths of Scripture to audiences of all ages and backgrounds, connecting with relevance and humor, but without sacrificing faithful exposition of the text. In *Beholding and Proclaiming*, Kristian lays out a simple process that anyone who communicates the Gospel can use to become a better, more effective communicator of the Scriptures. Whether you are just starting out or have been ministering for years, this book should be in your library. Study it. Work the principles. And watch God move."
- Matthew Rice, J.D.
Lead Pastor, Life City Church
Columbus, OH

"Preaching is no easy task precisely because telling a story— truthfully, compellingly, creatively and timely is no easy task. What we get in *Beholding and Proclaiming* is an extension of it's author. Kris takes his years of preaching experience, his humility of heart and the very fabric of his own story and offers us the tools to preach with our own lives. In a time where society is hungry for preaching that is imaginative and responsible, honest and truthful, timely and spirit-empowered, *Beholding and Proclaiming* will equip preachers of any context and in any circumstance to be an

instrument that ushers in God presence through God's preached word."
- Rich Pérez
Pastor of preaching and vision at Christ Crucified Fellowship
New York, NY

"Kristian gets that preaching is about more than explaining the text, but stirring the heart. It's about more than engaging the intellect, but engaging the mission. This book will do all of this for your own preaching, while empowering you to train the next generation of teachers"
- Andrew Mook
Founding pastor of Sanctuary Church
Providence, RI

The thing I love most about this book is that it's rooted in practice that's been refined over and over again. Kristian is not only a student of preaching, he is a preacher himself. So rather than approach the topic academically, he's approaching it practically from an urban context. Don't miss this!
- Daniel Im
Author of *No Silver Bullets*, coauthor of *Planting Missional Churches*, Director of church multiplication at NewChurches.com, and teaching pastor

"When you hear Kristian Hernandez preach, you can literally feel the heat of his burning passion for God. This it not mere affectation and style, but a genuine fire fueled by his prayer drenched devotional life. I am so glad that he writes the way he preaches, and that he addresses the heart of the preacher over and above the craft. Not that his craft is lacking in the least, but Kristian demands that the preacher beholds and cherishes God above all. Aspiring preachers should devour this little book. If followed closely, *Beholding and Proclaiming* will produce preachers like Kristian, the kind that will set themselves on fire with God's word and people will come to watch them burn."
- Dihan Lee,
Lead Pastor, Renew Church
Los Angeles, CA

Kristian Hernandez

CONTENTS

Endorsements i

1 Why A Book on Preaching 1

2 Devotionally 11

3 Exegesis 26

4 Christ 34

5 Redemptive Arc 43

6 Evangelion 51

7 Audience 64

8 Story 74

9 Expectation 83

10 Decrease 95

11 Word of Caution 98

WHY A BOOK ON PREACHING?

In many ways Christ has been pursuing me and reaching for me since I was in the womb. That's an odd thing to say, but it's the best way I can describe the origins of God's redemption in my life. I was born out of wedlock, the second child born as a result of an adulterous affair. My sister's birth caused such shame and turmoil in my father's life and marriage that when my mother was pregnant with me his decision was to have me terminated. He beat my mother so she would miscarry as well as took her to an abortion clinic three times while pregnant with me.

Each time my mother left the clinic in tears, unable to carry out the abortion. She would lie to my father and say it was taken care of. But as her belly continued to grow he grew suspicious and would then proceed to beat her and send her back to the clinic. Finally, the third time at the clinic a woman came and told her, "Don't abort this child. God has a plan for this child's life." She burst into tears, ran off and that night she was on a plane heading to Puerto Rico where eventually I was born. My dad was glad to finally have a son but died shortly after I was born. Christ rescued me before I had the ability to recognize his grace!

My actual Christ conversion began when I was 14 years old while smoking weed on a street corner with my good friend Will. Now between the ages of 10 and 14, it felt like I had lived a few lifetimes. I lost my virginity at the age of 10, began to smoke cigarettes and drink shortly after, was smoking weed by the age of 12, and was selling marijuana and, occasionally, crack cocaine by the age of 14. I was lost and numb in my soul, but on that street corner, I heard God speak to my heart as I saw Will's brother, Peter, walk across the avenue carrying a Bible. As a 14 year old kid standing on that street corner, I was unaware of how lost I was as the mayhem that began from the start of my life had slowly grown and was now suffocating me little by little.

1

Peter was one of the most popular guys in our neighborhood because of his dancing skills. Everyone wanted to hang out with him. At any given moment there would be 20 to 30 people swarming his house to see his new dance moves and just be around him because he was a cool guy. On that day while I hung out with his brother on the street corner, I was struck with the question, "What made him leave the life I am living, forsaking the money, respect and women I long for, to walk around with a Bible"? I didn't know the answer to that question yet, but as I saw a sense of peace on his face, the likes of which I had never seen before, I was struck with a sense of wonder.

I will never forget my first conversation with Peter. His eyes radiated the love of Christ. He wasn't religious or weird. He was down to earth, but when he opened the Scriptures to me it felt like God was speaking directly to my soul. He directed my attention to John 3:16-21. Even though I didn't go to church, I knew the words of John 3:16 since it was such a well known verse of Scripture. Mentally I understood that God loved the world and that he sent Jesus to this world because of his love, but I didn't understand this in my soul. I was not gripped or changed by that truth in the slightest. Despite my familiarity with John 3:16, I had never read or heard the words found in verses 17-21, but in particular verses 19-20. When Peter said the words "people loved darkness rather than the light because their works were evil," it was as if a veil was lifted from eyes and I was exposed to the darkness in my own soul. I realized at that moment the degree of shame I carried and how I would wait for the dark of night to do the crazy things we did in the streets. The invitation of Christ to be loved by him and to live in the light of his grace captured me that day!

On September 26, 1994, I confessed faith in Christ as Lord, and I put my trust in him for my forgiveness of sin and surrendered my life to him. From the moment I took my first breath as a Christian, I wanted to preach to the world. His salvation was so real to me! I knew I was formerly spiritually dead and Christ had made me alive. I was lost in my sin, and his grace lovingly rescued me. I have never been the same since that day.

The joy of Christ's love in my life thrust me into the streets of New York City searching for people to share the Gospel with. Growing up in Brooklyn you were taught to be tough and bold, or else you would get eaten alive, but I finally had something to be truly bold about! Though I was immature age wise, my love for Christ was insatiable, and thankfully, I wasn't alone in this love. My friends and I would go on the trains during our school break and preach to packed subway cars. We didn't get pastoral permission to go and preach because we didn't think a Christian needed permission to preach the Gospel, especially because Jesus had already commissioned us to go preach. Come to think about it, do people in love ask our permission to talk about the one who holds their heart? Never! They can't help but share about the person that has arrested their heart and it was the same for us.

This hunger to preach and teach became all-consuming. I devoured the New Testament as a teenager. At school I would skip lunch each day just to read my Bible. I actually failed some classes my first semester in high school because, in my immaturity, I thought I was being truly spiritual by only focusing on Scripture above formal scholastic learning. It was ignorant, but it was ignorance that was fueled by raw passion for God. Behind my drive to consume Scripture was a compelling need to be ready to share the Gospel, to answer the questions of the skeptics, to strengthen a struggling brother or sister in Christ. I wanted to know God and make Him known so I kept my face in his word.

Early on in my faith journey I found myself obsessed with studying the art and craft of preaching. I loved preaching, everything about it. A good sermon felt like music to me. The beauty and power that God would release through the preaching of his word captured me. I would hang around my pastor as much as I could and would grill him with questions. I would listen to sermons everyday, burning through many AA batteries as I listened with my Sony Walkman (if you don't know what that is like, it was an ancient technology called the "Cassette").

Soon I began to have opportunities to preach at our youth group or lead a small group at a friend's apartment and I fell in love with teaching and preaching even more. I loved the moment of delivering a message, but I especially the preparation for it. I would devote hours upon hours to study and prayer before preaching. It didn't matter if it was a small crowd or a large crowd, I would pray and prepare with a great intensity. When I wasn't preparing to preach, I was listening to great preachers and taking mental notes of how they handled passages of Scripture, their use of stories, their cadence and intensity. Looking back I realize now that I was slowly preparing for what would become my life's call as I grew older. Everything about preaching fascinated me. I wanted to push myself to learn how to preach with great spiritual power and authority because I saw firsthand the lives of people all around me transformed through the word of God.

As a young person I saw firsthand how the preaching of Jesus and his grace was powerfully changing people's lives. I came to faith in Christ at Resurrection Church in Sunset Park, Brooklyn. My pastor, Bishop Joseph Mattera, started this church with his wife, Pastor Joyce Mattera, at the height of the crack epidemic in the 80's. Our neighborhood was taken hostage by drugs, crime and poverty. In 2018 there are few real estate markets that can rival Brooklyn, with tons of people moving in and new luxury apartments popping up everywhere you turn, but when I was a kid people were running from Brooklyn! But as God often does, he chose to display his glory amidst the brokenness all around us and God used my pastors to start a church that would do just that. At our church I saw people who were addicted to drugs, entrenched in poverty, and had little hope that their circumstances would change receive new life in Christ and watched as the trajectory of their lives would shift. The Gospel would slowly begin to change every aspect of their lives, not just their souls. Many of these people would go on to obtain degrees, embark on amazing careers, start businesses and buy homes. The children of these men and women would grow up in homes that were radically different than the ones their parents were raised in - all because of Jesus.

Seeing people that were down and out receive hope and change through Christ was amazing, but seeing people encounter Jesus who were pretty comfortable and well adjusted in life fascinated me all the more. As someone who grew up around drugs and poverty, it was easy to imagine that people who lived in nice homes, went to great schools and had high-paying jobs didn't "need" Jesus as much as I needed him. That illusion was gloriously shattered as I saw people in our church who had comfortable lives encounter the reality of Jesus and were utterly transformed. When I saw people who had every earthly advantage we in the hood desperately needed lay down their lives before Jesus, recognizing how empty their lives were without Christ, I was utterly blown away.

This September 26th it will be 24 years since I first professed faith in Christ and I haven't stopped seeing God transform people through the power of his word. The church I pastor, Hope Astoria, is filled with people who have been broken by success and people broken through struggle. I have the privilege of seeing Christ transform both kinds of people. When ministry gets hard (as it often does), the joy of seeing God at work in people's lives fuels me to keep preaching, to keep declaring who God is and what he has done, and trust him to transform lives as only he can.

By now, it should be evident that I hold a high view of the word of God and the act of preaching, but I also hold a deep love for fellow pastors and preachers. Being a pastor is one of the toughest jobs in the world! To be clear, there are tough jobs out there that make being a pastor seem like a day in the park, but I would argue when you combine all the complexities of pastoring compared to other jobs, pastoring can easily take the trophy of toughest job. The hours are long, the expectations are high, the problems you work to address are complex, and the skills needed to thrive are many. As pastors we are entrusted with the sacred work of preaching and teaching God's word to people who desperately need it, but who often resist it. If that wasn't challenging enough, we are often dealing with our own struggles or situations with our families while, at the same time, we are pastoring others. Week in and week out, pastors find the courage to stand behind their pulpits and preach God's word as an act of obedience. With each passing year of pastoral ministry my admiration and love for pastors continues to grow!

My love for Christ, for his word preached and for preachers is what has moved me to write this book because quite honestly there is a crisis that is hitting the church! The crisis I'm referring to deals with 1) the low level of Gospel fluency among the people of God, 2) a need for training preachers at the local church level and 3) pastoral fatigue.

I write this book in the hopes of providing a helpful framework for people who want to get more from their study of Scripture, even if they never preach from a pulpit. As a pastor I find that one of the greatest needs among Christians is biblical literacy that leads to personal transformation and obedience. Yet most Christians don't regularly encounter God through his word in their own study, and sadly many sermons aren't adequately feeding the people of God. Among those who do read Scripture on their own, they are typically not studying Scripture in a way that digs deeply into God's word beyond discovering a nugget of wisdom here and there. Their reading of Scripture will remain at this level if they don't receive tools on how to go deeper into Scripture in a way that is Christ-centered and obedience-focused. Preaching in many churches won't become transformative apart from some help in these areas. If we don't address these issues, many Christians will only gain tons of head knowledge that is divorced from practical obedience, or they will walk away with a devotional nugget from a particular passage without ever knowing how to study the Scriptures as a whole. I hope this book can help address this need.

I also write this book for people who sense a call to ministry, but perhaps feel stuck on how to develop their gifts in that direction. For those for whom seminary is not an option in the near future, I hope this book will help bridge some gaps for you. As I write this book I think of the countless young leaders in the inner-cities of America and throughout the world who can't afford the luxury of formal theological education. I think of youth leaders who lead with great passion, but often lack substantive training. I think of my friends who are planting churches and would love a secondary preacher in their church, but either can't afford to hire someone or can't wait the many years it would take for someone to receive formal training away from their church. I hope this book can be used in church plants to train lay preachers of all ages to bless their churches in significant ways before they attend seminary.

I write this book with my pastor friends in mind who have expressed fatigue in connection to preaching week in and week out. These friends love the holy work of preaching. They are gifted, called and have seen much fruit with respect to preaching, but that doesn't mean they don't experience weariness. Many of them are pastoring young church plants that don't have the budget for guest speakers and they don't have well-trained secondary preachers to share the load, so with no other choice they plough through. From personal experience I have felt the fatigue that comes from preaching 17-20 Sundays in a row (some pastors I know preach many more weeks in a row). Even if there are periodic breaks, I know of many pastors that preach upwards of 45 Sundays a year. This kind of a preaching load concerns me because it's not sustainable over the long haul. I worry for my colleagues in ministry who can't take vacations, go on sabbatical or simply be able to show up to church and receive God's word for themselves from someone else. I hope this book can help provide a pathway to train lay preachers, who would not only preach powerfully, but also provide much needed rest to their pastors while blessing local churches with homegrown preachers.

But the greatest reason I write this book is...

Four percent. That's right, you are reading that correctly. The greatest reason for me writing this book is four percent, but four percent of what you may ask? Based on research conducted by Exponential (www.exponential.org), less than four percent of churches in America are reproducing churches, which he would define as churches that start other churches. Todd Wilson, in his book *Multipliers: Leading Beyond Addition*, gives us a harsh reality check. As I read this book it facilitated a clarifying moment for my life and ministry, and it helped to bring a renewed sense of purpose for the training of preachers.

Wilson highlights that despite having many megachurches in America, multi-site churches, church planting movements and the like, there is still an alarming problem before us: many of our most flourishing churches are focusing more on addition rather than reproducing through multiplication. Though these churches are adding more services, starting new campuses and maybe even planting other churches, the "scorecard" of ministry, Wilson argues, is still a scorecard that favors addition.

In all fairness, addition in ministry is not a bad thing. We should celebrate more lives being transformed, more baptisms, greater generosity, and the other meaningful metrics we track. The problem Wilson notes is the kind of ministry addition that fosters an accumulation of resources to one church over the lifespan of that one church without ever reproducing beyond itself. However big that church can become, it will one day fade away. The problem with this kind of addition is that it will never live into the future because it will be one-generational.

Unless something dramatically changes, 50 years from now we will be in serious trouble, let alone 100 years. With the increasing secularization of our culture and the high number of churches closing every year, it is really sad news that only four percent of churches reproduce in a multiplying manner. At best, we will barely hang onto the traction we are gaining in our cities. At worst, all of our efforts are akin to throwing a measly glass of water onto a four alarm fire.

For the purposes of framing this book, Wilson's argument sheds some important light on the need for local churches to lead the charge in training the next generation of preachers. Multiplying preachers is a crucial missing link for the Gospel to multiply in our cities. Until we begin to intentionally train preachers at the local church level, the multiplying of churches will continue to lag. What we need is to train preachers at a heightened pace that would allow us to make up for lost time. We need an intentional plan and tools to help bridge this gap.

The go-to strategy for the majority of churches has been to farm out the training of preachers to seminaries. As good as seminary training has served the church, it has also slowed down the training of preachers and the reproducing of churches. The time and expense it takes for a pastor to earn a seminary degree can create an unhelpful hurdle for the development of future leaders and multiplying churches. In addition, the training seminaries provide with respect to preaching seem to focus on a sole pastor preaching faithfully over their lifetime, rather than empowering the pastor to train many preachers over the course of their ministry. It's still rooted in an addition strategy.

Perhaps the greatest detriment of overly depending on seminaries to train the next generation of preachers is that local churches have abdicated their responsibility and lost sight of their role in the development of preachers. In our present reality, the people of God have been reduced to a crowd that is preached to rather than a community that incubates future prophets. Pastors are expected to preach week in and week out and are considered to be faithful to their job if they fill the pulpit the majority of Sundays, without any thought to what happens after they are gone.

With many pastors from the "Boomer" generation set to retire shortly, there are many churches facing the difficult truth that no one has been trained and developed in-house to carry the mantle of preaching into the future. Their only hope for the future of their church is to find a pastor from outside to come and serve or else their doors will close. Nothing inherently wrong with this approach, but it's important to be clear that in those situations it was the intentional training and development of a pastor through another church and ministry that saved the day for that church. Unless we begin to course correct on this matter, the pool of trained leaders won't begin to catch up to this growing need for trained pastoral leaders and this gap will only widen as the years go on.

Seminaries have trained countless pastors and thank God they have fulfilled this role as well as they have thus far. Responsibility for this crisis doesn't lie with them. The hard pill to swallow is that the people most responsible for why the Gospel isn't spreading and churches' aren't multiplying are us pastors. We bear disproportionate responsibility for the dearth of trained leaders.

The sad reality is that many of us pastors aren't determined to multiply preachers in our churches. Creating opportunities for developing preachers is not one of our priorities. The idea of sharing our pulpits with them is almost sacrilege. "They are not ready" we say. "Preaching is holy and only seasoned, godly, gifted people should be allowed to do so" we say. I don't disagree with those objections at all, but I think it's fair to say these objections can often conceal a dark motive, namely the desire to maintain our status and power.

Developing other preachers entails a certain death for us as pastors as we face the reality that we won't be around forever and that others could do what we do just as well as we do, and often better than us. I believe avoiding that death is at the heart of why we aren't multiplying preachers. Every time I have trained someone to preach and shared the pulpit with them I have had to face the feeling that people may connect more with them as a preacher than they do with me. In fact, on many occasions people have praised these developing preachers in ways that exacerbated those feelings. If my eyes are not fixed on glorifying Jesus and advancing his Kingdom rather than mine, the risk and pain involved in working yourself out of a job as a pastor is too heavy to bear. It would be far easier emotionally to not face our fears and our own finiteness, and as a result not commit to developing others.

All things considered, I would argue that the reasons to develop new preachers far outweigh any reservations we have, especially in light of the less than four percent of churches that are multiplying. There is an urgent need for pastors and churches to put their hands to this plow and reckon that the task of developing preachers falls on their shoulders. The baton of the ministry of preaching must be passed to the next generation. If that should fail to happen, we will bear much of the blame.

If for no other reason, I hope that our love for broken and lost people (souls that desperately need the Gospel) would motivate us to get our hands dirty and start this holy work!

I hope this book will provide a matrix to enable local churches to develop the next generation of preachers within their own context. My prayer is that God would use this book to unleash an army of preachers that will fearlessly proclaim the Gospel! From youth leaders who want to learn to preach, to home group leaders looking for tools to serve others well, to vocational pastors looking to grow themselves as well as seasoned pastors looking for ways to train others, may these words be used to spread the fire of God's love in our times!

HOW THIS MATRIX WORKS

The steps in this book are designed to help facilitate an encounter with God. That encounter will be the foundation of your sermon so that by the time you are preaching you will be communicating truths that have set your own soul on fire. You will be feeding people with what God has fed your own heart.

The preaching matrix you will learn in this book is communicated through the acronym DECREASE. Each letter represents an 8 step process that will empower you to faithfully preach God's word. I divide these 8 steps under the banner of two movements. These movements are BEHOLDING and PROCLAIMING.

What I'm proposing is to divide our sermon preparation into two parts. The first part is BEHOLDING, the second part is PROCLAIMING.

Steps 1 through 5 in this matrix represent the steps that allow us to BEHOLD the glory of God as revealed in Scripture. These steps are designed to help us to quite simply stare at God, feasting on his person.

Steps 6 through 8 are focused on the act of preaching. These steps help us to craft our particular message, as we do the work of translating into sermon form the glory of God you have been beholding.

My conviction is that preaching should be born from a posture of beholding the glory of Christ. We can't faithfully preach about what we have not beheld ourselves. But if we have truly gazed upon God, preaching of some kind or another will be the fruit because having stared at the glory of God, it's impossible to not speak freely of the wonder we behold.

Acts 4:18-20 says "Then they called them in again and commanded them not to speak or teach at all in the name of Jesus. But Peter and John replied, 'Which is right in God's eyes: to listen to you, or to him? You be the judges! As for us, we cannot help speaking about what we have seen and heard.'"

Did you catch that? "We cannot help speaking". What they saw and heard compelled them, empowered them, energized them to preach. If you preach regularly, I'm sure you know the difference between a sermon that you "couldn't help speak" versus a sermon that you felt obligated to preach because it was your responsibility to do so.

As we go through each step I hope you will gain new tools or sharpen existing ones that will help you to better behold the glory of God and proclaim that same glory in ways that will glorify God. With that said, let's start beholding the glory of God!

BEHOLDING

DEVOTIONALLY

How is God awakening your heart through his word?

EXEGESIS

What is the context of this passage?

CHRIST

How is this text understood in light of Christ?

REDEMPTIVE-ARC

How does this text fit within the meta-narrative of Scripture?

EVANGELION

How is the Gospel declared in this text? How do we interpret this text in light of the Gospel?

PROCLAIMING

AUDIENCE

What are the idols in peoples hearts that would resist the Gospel of Christ?

STORY

How will your sermon outline tell the story of God?

EXPECTATIONS

What does God expect people to do based on this sermon? What is your divine expectation as a preacher for this sermon?

DEVOTIONALLY

What I'm proposing in this book is not a new method, shortcut, or anything you haven't heard before. These concepts have been written about many times over, by much better writers and far better preachers than myself.

Before I begin to spell out the steps towards developing sermons, I think it's helpful to provide some context behind one of the biggest challenges faced when we set out to preach God's word. I wish this issue only existed in the broader culture, but sadly it is just as much a part of church culture. It's subtle, but it's always at work; unless we name it, we won't be able to confront it. What I'm speaking about is a culture that rushes our souls in the work of preaching.

Developing a sermon is a process that is best undertaken slowly, yet slow is the word least used by preachers to describe sermon prep. Most preachers feel rushed, never having enough time. The word of God rarely is given the proper time to marinate in our souls, robbing the preacher from receiving a nourishing gift for their own hearts, let alone allowing for a hearty feast to be prepared for the church. As a result, most sermons are akin to a microwaved meal. They are made quick, are barely healthy, and though they have the form of real food, it's not the same.

The time constraints on our lives are real. Whether bi-vocational, a lay leader, or a full-time vocational pastor, each of these stations in life have their respective challenges in creating time to prepare to preach. Simply leading our personal lives and families can be so time consuming, let alone the demands that come with ministry leadership. It's hard to create the necessary time for prayer, study and thought that developing a sermon requires. If you do manage to create time, the combined stress makes it close to impossible to engage in this work slowly. We are in a rush, always in a rush!

As someone who preaches upwards of 40-45 weeks a year, I fully understand the pressure of preaching regularly and the toll that this can take on one's soul. When faced with a looming preaching date, it's natural to rush and get to work on crafting a sermon. Whether you are a youth leader preparing for a meeting, a small group leader preparing to unpack a text in your home, or a lead pastor who preaches on a weekly basis, the pressure of a sermon deadline can cause havoc on all of us.

Thankfully there is a way forward, but it's not an easy road. Not only must we be willing to engage in the sermon development process in a much slower way, we must also be willing to commit to a much different approach than perhaps we are accustomed. I'm assuming that you want to take this plunge because otherwise you wouldn't be reading this book, so with that in mind, let's begin.

The first step in developing a sermon is not truly a step in that direction at all. In fact, it's kind of an anti-sermon step because in many ways this first step invites us to stop dead in our tracks rather than rush us toward finalizing a sermon. This first step is to approach the text of Scripture DEVOTIONALLY. This may sound so obvious and almost unnecessary to even state, but if you will indulge me, I hope to make a case that it's not so obvious. In fact, it's sorely missing in our day.

The starting place for all sermons is beholding the glory of God in the face of Jesus Christ, which is to say that prayerful devotion must precede proclamation. In essence the preacher shouldn't approach the word of God first and foremost to develop a sermon. Rather their approach to God's word should be worshipful devotion.

As basic a premise as this might be, in the current culture of preaching I dare say it's countercultural and borderline revolutionary. This is the sad reality: though the preaching and teaching of God's word proliferates pulpits, podcasts, books, and conferences, prayerful devotion has not grown in the church at a commensurate rate. Many Christians believe in God, but not many of them actually enjoy God and delight to be with him. The same can be said about those of us who preach and teach God's word. This is quite sick!

Though this appraisal sounds harsh and potentially judgmental, I write these words with a tear in my heart. To be truthful I have been in this dreadful place many times in my journey as a pastor. The constant vigilance of my soul is aimed at preventing my return there. So I write this as one who has suffered in that place and is aware that I can slip back into it if not careful, and please understand my words as fueled by empathy, not judgment.

In addition to being able to commiserate personally, I also interact with pastors and church planters on a constant basis. Many of them have confessed a lack of passion for God in their souls. That sort of confession can be difficult to admit to the leaders in their own churches. Often it's easier to admit to someone outside of their church and because they sense that I personally can understand, these pastors have often shared the true state of their hearts with me. Though I can deeply empathize with what they are describing, it's still hard to hear it.

Though all of this may sound very anecdotal, the statistics on pastoral burnout and moral failings attest to something rotting at the core. There is a sickness in the hearts of many preachers. I would argue that the lack of personal devotion to God is a major cause of this malady. The absence of devotion independent from the task of preaching has become so common that it hardly goes noticed in our lives. The results of this are seriously alarming.

We enter into a dangerous arena whenever preaching becomes disconnected from the life of God in the soul of the preacher. When this happens preaching slowly and subtly starts to become a performance rather than life-giving ministry. Our relationship with God as his children and as our father should always be the foundation of all preaching and ministry. When preaching doesn't flow from that starting point, God is reduced to a subject we are speaking about rather than the omnipotent being our hearts have been captured by.

You may be wondering "What's the big deal? There is an aspect of performing in any engaging communication and shouldn't preaching be engaging? You are such an alarmist!" The issue is not performance alone, but that performance has seemed to trump devotion as the foundation of preaching. When preaching descends to performance, a danger emerges: this kind of preaching can't nurture love for God in the church. It will only breed Christians after its own kind, namely performance-based Christians. Even if the doctrine is correct, the heart of this kind of preaching is severely off. If preaching is not proclaimed from a soul that is actively baptized by the fire of God's love, it is only intellectual ascent and lifeless ritual.

In life, there are few things as tragic as a loveless marriage. As a pastor I have walked with couples who struggled in their marriages for all sorts of reasons. Sometimes trauma and tragedy have impacted the marriage. What started out as a relationship marked by joy, passion and love devolves into a business relationship. It's painful. Though the road out of that rut can be hard, most couples choose to fight their way through because, deep down inside, they know this is not how things should be. They know marriage shouldn't be lifeless and joyless, so they decide to pursue mature passion.

Why am I referencing the dynamics of marriage when talking about preaching? The marriage between Christ and his church offers a vital image that informs the task of preaching. Ephesians 5:22-31 describes the relationship between Christ and his church as the relationship between a bridegroom and a bride. This passage paints a picture for us: Christ is engaged to his church, waiting till the end of the age when Revelation tells us he will be rewarded with the gift of his bride. Those of us who receive Christ and join his church are promised the ultimate reward, the reward of one day becoming his spouse, of having God commit to covenant faithfulness to us for all ages.

If you have ever been around an engaged couple that can't wait to get married, then you have tasted in small measure the passion that exists in the heart of Christ for his people. Christ purchased us with his very blood. You can't get more passionate than that! His love for his bride is red hot, unwavering and all-consuming. This is not a love of convenience or a passing interest, his love for us is the very definition of devotion.

Why is this relevant to preaching? Because the task of preaching is born in that intersection between Christ and the passionate love he has for his bride. The preacher is simultaneously a recipient of God's love and a herald of God's love. As preachers we are first recipients of God's love, and this empowers us to be conduits of that same love. The saying that "you can only give what you have first received" is perhaps truest for the preacher.

It's so crucial that devotion to God becomes and remains the starting place of all preaching. Ironically, this means that the beginning of a sermon doesn't have preaching as a goal at all. The birthing of a sermon takes place in a sort of "anti-sermon" space because, as we adore the living God, sermons become the last thing we're thinking of.

Devotion of this sort is akin to the bedroom chambers between a man and his wife. Lovers love to be alone. In those private, intimate moments their hearts connect. In the vulnerability of that space their souls meld together and passion is deepened, renewed and rekindled. What happens between them stays between them, and even if they shared details of those moments, they never share all the details. It's too sacred. It's too intimate. To disclose everything to others would violate the intimacy of those moments. It would be so foreign and even perverse for a couple to enter into that intimate space for the sole purpose of sharing the details with others.

Preaching that is not rooted in a hidden, private, intimate devotion of this kind has a tinge of that kind of perversion to it, regardless of how "biblically-based" it may be. The unfortunate truth is that many sermons are not birthed from a place of devotion, largely because we have reduced God as the content for our talks, rather than being the obsession of our souls. I wish I could say that I've stayed clear from this lifeless place myself. But unfortunately I have been there far too many times. There is nothing worse than delivering a sermon that is the product of an academic construal of theological concepts with a bit of entertainment mixed in. You can carry this out from a sincere place, with a heart that wants to glorify God and love his church, but in the end it's strange and antithetical to the very nature of our relationship with God.

We are in dire need of a serious course correction. This change is needed not just for the sake of the quality of sermons, but more for the very souls of preachers themselves! Many preachers are dying a slow death, one

Sunday at a time, one sermon at a time because their preaching is edging them further and further away from God their father.

Richard Foster in his book *Celebration of Discipline* shares truths vital to slowing down and fostering devotion towards God. All of the disciplines in his book are helpful towards that end. But I would like to focus on the disciplines of silence and fasting. Of these two disciplines, I will start with silence.

The spiritual discipline of silence is crucial in fostering devotion to Christ. In silence we are reminded that our posture in God is first and foremost one of receiving, not giving. We don't add anything to God, therefore silence roots us in the essence of the gospel. The gospel proclaims that God in Christ has come to us, seeking us, not for what we can give, but because we desperately need what God offers us in his grace. When we enter into silence before God we are reminded of this truth as we come simply to behold God. In silence we contemplate who God is and what God has done. When our hearts are silent, we still our souls and ready ourselves to hear his "still small voice" as Elijah did at the mount.

As we consider the necessity of silence in order to meditate on the word of God, it's necessary to note the difference between Eastern meditation and Christian meditation. In Eastern meditation the goal is to empty one's mind and allow the universe to fill it. There is no filter in this kind of meditation. Whatever we receive is considered as a good gift from the universe without applying any discernment or judgment on it. This is the point of departure for us: unlike Eastern meditation, for us Christians truth is rooted in the idea that there is a benevolent, transcendent God who reveals himself in Christ. In light of this definitive and distinct revealing of God, we as Christians are always comparing and contrasting all "truths" against who Christ is.

The famed preacher George Whitefield, who was instrumental in the Great Awakening that swept through America, shared some profound words regarding silence. Whitefield once said: "Whole days and WEEKS have I spent prostrate on the ground in silent or vocal prayer." Days and weeks! What an awe-inspiring description of prayer.

Preaching that is not born in silence lacks power, and the preacher's soul that is not nurtured in silence isn't humbled enough to carry the weight of the word of the Lord. It's in silence that we hear the powerful thunder of God's voice in our own souls. When we disconnect from our loud and clamorous world, we liberate ourselves from the echo chambers of life. It's in this stillness that we cultivate listening hearts and can come to hear God's voice through the illumination of his word. In silence God's word is absorbed in our lives and is received, not as knowledge or theory but as the life-giving bread that it truly is.

Silence is a precious commodity in our world. The constant noise from blaring earphones, news feeds, social media and our phones is staggering. If you live in a crowded city like I do, silence is really rare, but the truth is that the suburbs and even the country are no strangers to boisterous noise. It's everywhere, because the noise of life takes residence in all of our hearts.

Augustine described our hearts as a "hissing caldron of desire". What an image! We could be completely alone in a monastery and yet find that our hearts are filled with noise. Our hearts are often stuffed to the brim with restless clutter. Our desires and the distractions accompanying them are much to contend with, especially given that God chooses not to compete with them at all. As God, he deserves our attention and expects us to silence our souls in order to listen to his voice. So if we are expecting God to raise his voice above the clatter, then we can keep waiting, because it won't happen. He waits for us to still our hearts and wait on him.

Sometimes this lack of silence is less about our physical location or the state of our hearts, and more to do with the season of life we are in. As a parent of three children under the age of nine, I can tell you that silence is a rare thing in my life. Disrupted sleep, constant demands, ever fluctuating schedules, managing sickness and everything in between makes cultivating silence a challenge. If it's not home life with kids, our careers often come with a frenetic pace leaving only small bits of room for silence or solitude.

The challenges to cultivating the practice of prayerful silence are many. Many of us choose to live without this practice, yet the danger to our souls from lack of silence is too great for us to ignore. So I ask you: how are you going to cultivate silence in your life? What are the margins of time that you could devote to silence? What time in your daily and weekly schedule can God expect you to come and meet him in silence? Without creating this rhythm of silence, developing fiery devotion for God will not be possible.

I remember when I first came to Christ as a 14 year-old kid. The sweetness of prayer in those early days! I couldn't get enough! I was present at almost every morning prayer meeting, every late night vigil, every weeknight corporate prayer gathering, and yet I craved for more. Though I loved to pray and be in the company of other believers who also enjoyed seeking God, there was nothing like learning to be alone with God. The problem I faced was that everywhere I turned all I found were people!

My mom, sister and I lived in a small, one bedroom apartment in Sunset Park, Brooklyn. I need to emphasize small! I remember the bathroom sink to this day because it barely stood above my knees; I had to bend down quite a bit to wash my face. The toilet was flush between the wall and the cast iron tub so much that your knees would hit either the wall or the tub. One person barely fit in that old bathroom.

You might be wondering, "why is Kristian talking so much about this bathroom?" or "what does this have to do with one's devotional life?" Those are keen questions to ask. Quite simply: for the first four years of my Christian faith that bathroom was my prayer closet! Yep, you read that right, the bathroom was my prayer closet!

As a teenager I would lock myself up in that bathroom and pace back and forth and kneel in that narrow space. It was awkward, not ideal, but it was so precious! I would encounter God in powerful ways. I would weep in God's presence, I would read Scripture and pray God's word, and I would wait in silence. Occasionally I would have to exit the bathroom while my mom or sister used it, and sometimes that meant I couldn't enter in immediately after, but that's besides the point!

The other place I would go to pray was Third Avenue. Now in those days Third Avenue was not an ideal place for prayer. In fact, the only thing that avenue was known for was drugs, prostitution, broken-down cars left on the side of the road, and pollution from the overpass that connected the Verrazano Bridge to the BQE. Though not an ideal place to cultivate the discipline of prayerful silence, it was during two-mile walks on Third Avenue that I learned to still my heart before God and listen. Occasionally I would talk to God audibly, but that had to be at selective times when no one was around so that people wouldn't think I was crazy. Engaging in prayerful silence and worship in the face of drug dealers, prostitutes and the abandoned scene that was Third Avenue had a profound impact on my soul. It was teaching me to never divorce my relationship with God from the fallen nature of our world and to develop a conscious dependence on the Holy Spirit in the midst of brokenness.

These days cultivating silence is much different for me. I'm a proud father of three beautiful children. Though I love them deeply, caring for them makes prayer really challenging. I have to wake up super early in order to pray and study God's word before they get up, or I have to stay up late in the night after they go to bed. Unlike most New Yorkers, I love long commutes on public transportation or in my car because it gives me a chance to study and pray without the typical demands and distractions of life.

I try to clean the living room, kitchen and bathroom at least once a week. Before anyone could pat me on the back for being a husband who cares for the physical state of my home, I will admit this is entirely a selfish act! Sure I love my wife and kids as I do this, and sure my wife is grateful for all the help that I give, but that's not the reason I do this. I clean those spaces because I have found that praying while cleaning comes easy to me. I am able to talk to God and listen to his voice while washing dishes or cleaning the living room. At times I play worship music while cleaning to help recenter my heart on God. These practices are a far cry from the ways of the desert fathers, but they have served me well in this season of life.

I share these stories because they are dear to me; remembering them stirs my soul. They help me to never forget the simplicity of devotion to God. I also share them in the hopes of encouraging anyone who may think silence can only be achieved at a monastery or in the woods. If you can get to those places, by all means go and enjoy their beauty! But if you can't, don't fret or consider yourself at a disadvantage because God can help you cultivate prayerful silence right where you are.

The second discipline Richard Foster speaks of is the discipline of fasting. Fasting from food for the sake of cultivating devotion towards God is never fun. In fact, I utterly hate it! I have never looked forward to fasting as something that I totally enjoy (like other things in life). Despite the benefits fasting yields, it is impossible to receive its benefits without passing through the grid of pain embedded in this discipline.

Writing about fasting is a tricky thing because Scripture tells us that we should not fast to gain the approval and praise of others. In fact, Scripture teaches us that any spiritual reward associated with fasting is lost when we engage in this discipline with the motives of pride or self-aggrandizement. So as I write about fasting, it would be dishonest for me to act like I don't engage in this discipline, but it would be prideful if I wrote about this in a way that was self-focused. It's a tricky line to walk, but because this is so important I'm willing to give this a go.

Foster writes about how the church engaged in fasting throughout the ages. He shares how it was a common practice of Christians to engage in 24-hour periods of fasting that would begin after lunch followed by fasting dinner and then fasting breakfast and lunch the following day. He shares how Christians would often fast in order to store up food and then would pool together that food to host banquets during which fellowship with other Christians would take place. But most importantly they would feed the poor and hungry through these means. Foster also shares how John Wesley and the ministers he trained held to the discipline of fasting Wednesdays and Fridays of every week. These are only bullet points of Foster's wonderful chapter on fasting. I hope it's enough to stir you to pick up the book and read it for yourself. But more importantly I hope it stirs you to consider personally engaging with the discipline of fasting yourself.

Reading of Wesley's discipline to fast gripped my heart as a young Christian who aspired to preach God's word. Something of this discipline felt right and good, though clearly there is nothing expressly written in the word of God that a minister should fast a certain number of days each week. To suggest or impose fasting in that kind of way would be a form of legalism.

Because there is profound wisdom in the discipline of regular fasting in the life of a minister, I raise this point not to say that you should fast a certain number of days a week or a year, but I do encourage you to take self-inventory. If you aren't fasting regularly this is something you should seek to address immediately.

Fasting doesn't make us holy, or cause us to earn favor with God. This discipline should not be a standard by which we judge our own maturity or the maturity of others. Fasting doesn't get God to do anything or obligate him to answer any prayers. So then, why fast? If all the sacrifice and inconvenience doesn't earn you spiritual cred with God, why should we do it?

My biggest argument for fasting is centered on the grace of God. If the grace of God in Christ has changed our lives and impacted our souls, if the grace of God that can't be earned or deserved has made us alive from sin and death, then fasting should be a natural byproduct of our lives. Why you may ask? I argue if a person is firmly rooted in the grace of God, fully clear and assured they can't add or take away anything from the free, saving grace of Christ, then that person should seek to engage in any and all spiritual disciplines that would allow them to feast on God's grace in greater measure. Fasting is one of those disciplines that allows us to savor his grace so deeply by the sheer fact it creates greater margin for prayer and study of his word through the time we gain from not eating food. In addition, fasting directs our physical appetites and our natural craving for food to find solace and satiety in God's presence and word alone.

I wish I could share specifics about the personal rhythms of fasting in my life, but I value my reward before God too much to get into all that (Matthew 6:16-18). I hope it's enough to hear me say that fasting has expanded my love for God, has re-centered me in God and has been a catalyst in the hands of God for amazing spiritual breakthroughs in my life and the life of our church. With the help of the Spirit of God, grounded in the word of God, everyone is free to develop their own rhythms of fasting in their lives. Have fun and get creative as God leads you, but for the sake of God's glory and your own personal feasting upon God's grace, I implore you not to give yourself an excuse if you are not regularly fasting.

How is God tugging at your heart as you read these words? Have you sensed his invitation to go away with him and be alone? My prayer is that you haven't made it to this point without having directed your heart to God in prayer, putting the book down to simply be with God. But if you have made it this far and haven't sought God, now is your time!

Find a time and place in your day to get alone with God. If you are a preacher and your Sunday sermon is looming before you, could I ask you to put that aside for the moment, create space for prayer and simply pour out your devotion before God. Give yourself full permission to enjoy God for God's sake alone and don't fret over your sermon. If your sermon is not birthed from a place of worshipful devotion, it's not going to mean much anyway!

Perhaps while reading this chapter you have come to realize your heart has grown cold and distant from God, even though you are actively serving his people through preaching and teaching. The descent from worshipfully proclaiming God's truth to performing sermons that are disconnected from devotion can happen to the best of us. Don't beat yourself up, but refuse to stay in that space for another second. Drop to your knees and cry out to God!

As you enter this prayerful space, reach for your Bible and open the word of God again, but this time do it ever so slowly and gently. You do this all the time to prepare for sermons, but this time you aren't going to God's word for that purpose. As you meditate on God's word, allow yourself the joy of feasting on his goodness and relish on the revelation of himself to us through the Scriptures. Savor every bite, chew on every promise, and bask in the goodness of God extending to you through his word.

Haddon Robinson in his book *Biblical Preaching* says that we must first encounter God as his child before we think about how we should preach God's word. In this moment, God is inviting you to lay down your title, your leadership, your responsibilities and give yourself permission to be his child. Crawl up in your heavenly father's lap and allow his love to envelop you, to heal you, and to capture your heart.

The starting place of all sermons is the place of devotion. But if you have heeded God's invitation to come and seek him and enjoy his presence then a sermon is the last thing on your mind right now! You are in a sacred place, a place only known by lovers of God. Soak in every moment in the holy presence of God and let his glory restore your soul and arrest your heart towards himself.

Like many things in our spiritual journey with Christ, the way forward requires a return to ancient practices, to the timeless disciplines God hands down to us through his word and through the lives of the saints of old. For starters we should take a good look at the practice of Lectio Divina.

Lectio Divina is the practice of reading Scripture for the sake of savoring the person of God. It's a slow process intended to bring the reader of God's word into contact with the essence of God. It's not an academic examination of Scripture. Lectio Divina is not a tool for developing sermons, it is a tool intended to slow down our hearts long enough for us to encounter God through his word. We are invited to receive God, not reduce him.

There are many resources on how to practice Lectio Divina so I won't expound on that here. But I will share a resource from my friends John and Kara Kim, pastors of The166 (www.the166.org), a micro church in Hell's Kitchen. Of all the various forms of Lectio Divina that are available, I personally find their format to be the most helpful.

If Lectio Divina is a new concept for you, I would highly encourage you to explore this discipline and begin to implement it slowly. It's a rich practice that takes some time to fully orient oneself toward. It's simple and profound, but a bit counterintuitive to the way most of us have been taught to engage with Scripture. As a result, my advice would be to give yourself time and embrace it slowly. It's rare that it yields immediate fruit, but over time it produces mature fruit in our souls.

I know you have a sermon to prepare for. Sunday is right around the corner, the worship team needs your notes, the slide presentation needs content, etc. The tyranny of the urgent is at work, even as you prepare to preach. Despite all that, can I ask you to ignore all of it and just sit with God and his word? Just sit and be with God. As hard as this may be in light of pressing demands, don't stop seeking God in this manner until you begin to find delight. The people to whom you are about to preach deserve a preacher that loves to be with God more than they love to speak about God, and more importantly God deserves a preacher that loves being his child above being a communicator.

Though there is still so much road to travel towards the preached word, you are on a good path now because you are facing God himself. Savor his presence!

Application:

1. Before you take on your preaching assignment, spend some time meditating on these passages and allow God to move your heart and soul towards him.

Psalm 27:3 One thing I ask from the Lord, this only do I seek: that I may dwell in the house of the Lord all the days of my life, to gaze on the beauty of the Lord and to seek him in his temple.

Psalm 27:8 My heart says of you, "Seek his face!" Your face, Lord, I will seek.

Mark 1:35 Very early in the morning, while it was still dark, Jesus got up, left the house and went off to a solitary place, where he prayed.

2. Open up the passage you will be preaching from and sit with it in prayer. Wait in God's presence with this passage on hand and a journal, and write down what grabs you from the passage. Are there any keywords or phrases

in the text? Is there an image offered in the text that draws your attention?

3. Are there any words that are repeated in the text? If so, what are they?

On the next pages you can check out the template for Lectio Divina that my friends at The166 have created.

Lectio Divina

Colossians 3:16: "Let the word of Christ dwell in you richly."
Hebrews 4:12: "For the word of God is alive and active."

Lectio Divina is a Latin term that means "divine reading" and it is a slow and reflective way of engaging the Scripture so that you can really open yourself up to what God wants to say to you. It is an ancient monastic practice that was first established in the sixth century by Saint Benedict. In Lectio Divina, you are basically taking a passage in the Bible and reading it over and over again and really soaking it in. As an analogy, it is like how a cow chews partly digested food, regurgitates it and chews it again and again until it gets digested. The process of Lectio Divina will definitely require you to slow down and be patient as you literally chew on the Bible passage. It involves reading a selected passage 3-4 times, where each reading is followed by different activities to help you connect with God.

Use the simple acronym T.I.M.E. to help you remember the process of Lectio Divina.

First prepare your heart to encounter God through His Word. Sit in silence, take a few deep breaths and ask the Holy Spirit to come and guide you.

1) TEXT - (Objective Focus) - Read the passage slowly and aloud for the first time and let the words sink in. Take the next two minutes of silence (or however long or short you want) to identify key words or phrases that strike you. This portion of Lectio Divina asks, "What are the main ideas of the passage?" This is the time for a studied examination of the passage when you identify the objective dimensions of its meaning. You can read commentaries and look up meanings of words if you wish.

2) IMMERSE (Subjective Focus) - Read the passage slowly and aloud for the second time. Take the next few minutes of silence to meditate on what the passage personally means for you. While the first reading sought the text's objective meaning, now we are reflecting on subjective meanings and personal associations that come to mind. Use your sanctified imagination to enter into the text: What do you see, feel, hear as you enter the scene? What are you feeling as you read the text? What personal longing is God speaking into? God may give you a picture or a living (rhema) word at this time. Take what God gives you and unpack it. Explore it with him.

3) MINISTRY (Prayer & Response) - Read the passage slowly and aloud for the third time. Take the next few minutes of silence to see what prayers emerge and stir up within you based on the previous two movements. What is God inviting you into through this text and how will you respond? Pray them out to the Lord. The goal here is intimacy with God so this may be a time to simply dialogue with him, to wrestle with him or to do something he asks you to do.

23

4) ENCOUNTER (Resting) - You can read the passage for the fourth time if you would like. It's optional at this point. During these last few moments of silence, simply dwell in God's presence and rest in what he said to you. This is the time to let God's living word soak into you for your ongoing formation.

The above guideline for group Lectio Divina can easily be adapted to individual practice. When doing Lectio Divina individually, the process can be more fluid and flexible. You may feel led to jump back and forth from one movement to another as the Holy Spirit leads.

On the next page you can find a sample of this Lectio format with a passage of scripture and some guidelines on how to prayerfully engage with the text.

Romans 5:1 Therefore, since we have been justified through faith, we have peace with God through our Lord Jesus Christ, 2 through whom we have gained access by faith into this grace in which we now stand. And we boast in the hope of the glory of God. 3 Not only so, but we also glory in our sufferings, because we know that suffering produces perseverance; 4 perseverance, character; and character, hope.5 And hope does not put us to shame, because God's love has been poured out into our hearts through the Holy Spirit, who has been given to us. 6 You see, at just the right time, when we were still powerless, Christ died for the ungodly. 7 Very rarely will anyone die for a righteous person, though for a good person someone might possibly dare to die. 8 But God demonstrates his own love for us in this: While we were still sinners, Christ died for us. 9 Since we have now been justified by his blood, how much more shall we be saved from God's wrath through him! 10 For if, while we were God's enemies, we were reconciled to him through the death of his Son, how much more, having been reconciled, shall we be saved through his life! 11 Not only is this so, but we also boast in God through our Lord Jesus Christ, through whom we have now received reconciliation.

1) TEXT - (Focus on the Objective) - Make observations on an objective level. What keywords or phrases strike you? What are the main ideas of the passage?

2) IMMERSE (Focus on the Subjective) - Meditate on what the passage personally means for you. What are you feeling as you read the text? What personal longing is God speaking into? Take whatever living (rhema) word God gives you and explore it with Him.

3) MINISTRY (Prayer & Response) - What is God inviting you into through this text and how will you respond? This may mean just sitting on it for a while, dialoguing with God or doing something that he asks of you. The goal is engaging with God towards more intimacy.

4) ENCOUNTER (Resting) - Simply dwell in God's presence and rest in what God spoke to you. This is the time to let God's living word soak into you for your ongoing formation.

EXEGESIS

Exegesis is the next step in the DECREASE process. By the end of this chapter I hope to explain what this word means and its place in preaching biblically sound messages.

But before I do so, allow me to share some of my personal journey. I hope it encourages you. After sharing my story we will come right back to the purpose at hand, namely discussing a process whereby we can work towards proclaiming the word of God and training preachers who do the same.

I remember as a teenager hearing the Bible described as God's love letter to humanity. Something about that description felt so weird, yet so right. What felt weird had much to do with my flawed view of God when I first professed faith in Christ as a teenager. I struggled to believe that God was fully loving, especially when I sinned against him. It was marvelous for me to hear that God demonstrated his love for me in that Christ died for me as a sinner, but it also seemed incomprehensible on some level. God loving a broken sinner who couldn't tell up from down made sense, but God loving one of his followers through the ups and downs of sanctification was really tough for me. The Bible felt like so many things to me, but seeing it as a love letter didn't compute during those times.

At the core of those struggles was that my faith in Christ did not rest on his perfect obedience, sacrificial death, and the righteousness he imputed to me by faith. My faith rested on my imperfect obedience and the mercurial state of my heart. When I was spiritually hot for God, I would soar like an eagle. But when my soul would run back to my idols, I would wallow in my sin and had no answer for my struggles. I couldn't reconcile God loving me during those low points. This false view of God resulted with me running from God and resisting his loving grace after I sinned. God's kindness would call me to repentance, but my false view of God would ignore his call.

For many years I struggled through a form of spiritual depression at the hands of this blockage. My heart couldn't wrap itself around the grace of God. This depression didn't just impede a private spirituality, it actually halted my entire life, impacting my grades in school, my relationships and even my physical health. I walked around miserable because I couldn't please God and couldn't grasp God loving me during those struggles. Though my heart was filled with gratitude towards God's mercies on my life, I felt so much despair when I considered how I continued to dishonor God in my thoughts, attitudes and actions.

The intensity of this struggle began when I was finishing high school. During my senior year it felt like I fell in a deep pit. If I could compare my knowledge of God to a ladder that could pull me out of that pit, I discovered that my knowledge of God was akin to a tiny ladder and I was sunken in a massive crater. My view of God was anemic in the face of my rampant disobedience.

As I've shared prior, I came to Christ when I was 14 years old, one month into my freshman year of high school. The fires of God's love swept through me and turned my world upside down from day one. Over the next three years my love for God grew, and my obedience to God seemed to increase daily. Sinful habits appeared to vanish in the blink of an eye. I developed a strong prayer life and devoured the Scriptures daily. I served in so many ministries and loved every second of it. I was discovering my gifts and using them in worship to Christ. Those first three years of my walk with God were truly amazing!

Unbeknownst to me, spiritual pride and legalism were brewing in my heart during this incredible season of "obedience" and "growth". Though sincere at the time, I now know that I wasn't truly walking in obedience or growing spiritually because, though the fruit of sin was disappearing from my life, under the surface I was actually nurturing the roots of sin in my heart. My obedience was not in response to the grace of God or fueled by the power of God through the Gospel. I came to find out during my senior year of high school that it was fueled by pride and a deep anxiety I held about God's love. Deep down inside I didn't fully believe God loved me of his own choosing, but that I was constantly earning or un-earning his love. With each act of obedience I was subconsciously building a case for why God should love me. I was obeying in order to earn God's love, rather than obeying because I was gripped and transformed by God's gracious love. Though outwardly my walk with God looked fruitful, I was watering the seeds of death in my soul. By my senior year of high school I could no longer ignore the true state of my heart.

Sexual lust and spiritual pride seized my life during senior year. I found myself powerless to do anything against them. I discovered that the progress I thought I made in the area of my sexual brokenness was only surface deep and that underneath the layers of my soul lay a brokenness I wasn't fully prepared to face. Though I opened up my heart to the grace of God and experienced incredible transformation on so many levels, I came to realize that I had not fully exposed the rawness of my heart to God. Powerful childhood memories and urges had been managed (at best) and now I couldn't suppress them any longer.

Part of my journey is that I lost my innocence rather young. I was exposed to sexually explicit movies and images when I was around six or seven. This challenged my ability to view females as sisters or friends. Simple childhood activities were no longer simple. I became sexually active at the age of 10, and because I looked older and was tall, I was hanging out with kids who were in their late teens. This was a recipe for disaster because with each friendship and each encounter with girls my chances of easing my way back into childhood were growing dim.

At this point you may be wondering, what does any of this have to do with exegesis? I share this part of my journey in conjunction with the concept of exegesis in order to highlight why a purely academic view of exegesis hurts our souls, let alone our preaching. The process of exegesis is akin to a shovel used in the service of excavation work. As we begin to dig deep into the text, the goal is not to emerge with solely head knowledge or facts. But as we dig deeper, the truths we discover and the truths that become clearer should not only inform our minds, but they are tools in God's hand to heal out hearts.

The term exegesis has been given a bad wrap of sorts. It's been robbed of its true beauty. Exegesis has been overwhelming described in an academic light, diverting it's aim away from our hearts, solely focusing on our minds. There is nothing inherently wrong in describing exegesis in an academic manner, yet by doing so we lose some of the beauty embedded in this process.

Exegesis means "to bring out". With respect to Scripture, exegesis is the work of interpreting and expositing a text. We explore the context of a biblical text by understanding the historical setting of the passage, the grammar of the text, as well as understanding the literary type of the passage we are studying. Exegesis helps us to bring out the meaning embedded in a text as we seek to apply God's truth to our lives.

Through exegesis we are first seeking to understand the author's intent to the particular audience they were addressing. We want to understand why it was written and what it meant to the first people hearing it. As we come to a text of Scripture, we are "bending our mind to the text," as Haddon

Robinson says, rather than bending the text to our minds and forcing it to say something it wasn't when first written.

Have you ever walked into the middle of a conversation? Perhaps you entered at the halfway mark of a story. That can be such an awkward situation! You want to participate in the conversation but you don't have context so you don't know where to begin. Walking into a conversation toward the tail end of a joke is another "fun" thing to do as you then become a bystander. Everyone erupts in laughter and you can't fully join in. The best you can do in those moments is take a listening posture and try to quickly understand what was shared before you arrived. After you introduce yourself to anyone you may not know, you are on your way to start some investigatory work. Once the pleasantries are exchanged, you can now ask the burning question "what are you all talking about"? Without immersing yourself in the context and backstory of those moments, your interjections will likely seem awkward and disruptive.

Exegesis is akin to walking into an existing conversation. God is a speaking and self-revealing God. Through exegesis we enter into the conversation he is having with his people. Our goal is to seek to understand God in the context of the people and the world that he was speaking to when Scripture was written. This process seeks to grasp the meaning of Scripture before we seek to derive the application of the text. We don't want to rush to application by speeding past the meaning of the text. We will easily misunderstand important things unless we take time to understand the original recipients and their context as God spoke to them. The misunderstandings that will ensue will be similar to when interjecting yourself into an existing conversation.

The opposite of exegesis is eisegesis. Contrary to exegesis, which seeks to bring out the meaning within the text, eisegesis imposes our own views and presuppositions onto the passage. Rather than bending our thoughts to the text, eisegesis bends the text to our thoughts. When this happens there is a danger we will miss, ignore or even resist God's true message to us while putting forth our own message as the word of God.

Biblically sound exegesis is sorely needed in our times! Sadly, the word of God is increasingly relativized to the standards of our culture. As this continues to happen, God is no longer worshipped as he truly is, rather he is worshipped as we have made him to be. Unless we acknowledge this and repent, we will find ourselves worshipping a god after our own image rather than worshiping the true God as revealed in Christ Jesus his Son. Instead of entering into an existing conversation that God is having through his word, we find ourselves creating conversations that God never had, ascribing to God ideas he never proclaimed. We attribute to God our modern values rather than interpreting and challenging our modern values in light of the word of God.

Exegesis helps ensure we don't obscure God's grace and truth. It helps us to be comforted by God as well as offended by God, and we sorely need both. It challenges our presuppositions and calls us to engage God as he reveals himself in his word, not as we wish he would be. Clearly it has an academic aspect to it, but it's a real blessing to us when some of the intellectual clutter can be set aside so that our hearts may gaze upon the glory of God. Exegesis, when truly engaged in, should do more than expand our minds, it should revolutionize our hearts!

Though my heart resisted at first, had I not engaged in the process of exegesis I would have never understood that the Bible is in fact God's love letter. Tragically, the years my heart was blind to God's heart towards me caused my soul to remain broken. Through exegesis I came to see God's character in a clearer light. As I dove deeper into Scripture, God's word journeyed from my head to my heart, transforming my mind and soul. Scripture not only renewed my mind, it warmed my heart.

As a married man of 11 years, I know all too well how easy it is to take something my wife says out of context, and vice versa. How quickly we can find ourselves down the path of a fight, forgetting that ultimately we love each other and are each other's biggest supporters. When we disconnect the words we speak from the context of the clear love we have for each other, a fight is likely to ensue. Exegesis helps us to place God's word in the proper context of his character as revealed in Scripture. Through his dealings with his people and the circumstances of their times, we come to see God as he truly is and come to see ourselves in the light of his character.

Ephesians 2:8 says we are saved by grace through faith. I have heard this so many times over the years, and shared it with others. But for so long I didn't understand it. This lack of rootedness was evident by how up and down my walk was. If I was faithful to God, then I perceived God to be faithful to me, but if I sinned against God, I imagined God would disown me. Every relational rejection I had experienced in my life told me that my logic made sense and that God could be no different. Though my heart wanted to believe God was different and though verses of Scripture indicate that God relates to me on the basis of grace, in the face of personal disobedience my understanding of grace crumbled.

It took some time, but I will never forget the moment when my heart began to understand the grace of God! I understood the concept devotionally, but my spiritual issues required an overhaul of my soul, not just a warming of my heart. It wasn't enough for my heart to be moved by the idea of God's grace; I needed to understand it so deeply that it would revolutionize how I saw God and how I saw myself.

This moment came during a time of prayer in my apartment. It was a Saturday, and oddly enough, I had the apartment to myself for many hours. My heart was heavy that day as my prayer became a cry of desperation to God. My prayer was for freedom from this bondage to an up-and-down spirituality. The spiritual depression was too much to bear so I cried out to God for freedom. I didn't have a predetermined view of what freedom would look like, so I was shocked by how my heart was emancipated that day.

As I prayed, the letter to the Ephesians came alive and the words "in Christ" leapt off the page. I had studied these words countless times, but while reading them this day throughout Ephesians, they finally made sense. I came to see that Christ was not only living in my heart through faith, but that I was living in Christ, placed in Christ by God the Father. This was life-altering truth because now I understood how the righteousness of Christ was imputed to me. I could finally see how God could love me unconditionally, even when my obedience was spotty, to say the least. I saw that God was not relating to me based on my obedience, but that he was relating to me based on the perfect, final, complete obedience of Jesus. In light of this letter and many other texts of Scripture, I came to see that my relationship with God was not built on the shifting sands of my own heart, but on the rock that is God's love and grace as given in Christ. I understood that God would not run from me in my sin because to do so would be to run from his own Son, his perfectly obedient Son whom I was now graciously placed in. I was the recipient of his grace, because I deserve none of it. He would treat me better than my personal obedience would ever warrant. God would always be good, even when I wasn't, and I would taste of his goodness in a ceaseless manner all because of Jesus.

A burden lifted that day, never to return! Since then I would love to tell you that I have sinned less, but in actuality I have sinned quite a bit more (or maybe I am just better at recognizing my own sin). What has changed is that I now repent quicker. To my continual shock and horror, I am constantly surprised by the depths of my sin and the depravity of my heart. On my own I don't naturally want God or his ways. I resist his love constantly, and I suffer the consequences of those choices. What has changed, and oh my goodness has it changed, is the realization that God is not running from me every time I sin! God is not tolerating me, he is madly in love with me and through Christ he has made provision for me to feast on his love, even when my heart would choose to wander. Rather than run from God in fear and shame, I now run to God in faith and expectation that his love is greater than my sin and that Christ's obedience is stronger than my disobedience.

If the first step in developing a sermon is devotionally reading the Scripture, then the second step of exegesis should be engaged with the intent of deeply understanding who God is and what he is saying. Through exegesis the goal is to help our minds understand how and why God's truth moved our hearts during our devotional reading of Scripture. Exegesis helps us to rightly discern what God is saying to us, what he is inviting us to understand about himself. In essence, exegesis is intended to help us fully receive God's love in all its truth, as offensive and comforting that may be.

Exegesis takes the seed of God's word and helps to drive it into the granite of our souls. This step transforms the lifeless soil of our hearts into fertile ground. Exegesis most certainly prepares us to preach, but first and foremost it invites us more fully into the light of God as we behold God's character and person more fully. The darkness of lies and subjective feelings about God give way to the eternal revealing of his character.

Engaging in exegesis in a way that engages both mind and heart will cause our sermons to better reveal the character and person of God. The temptation to be culturally relevant as a preacher is so strong that if we are not careful we will seek to be liked and accepted by our hearers at the expense of prophetically revealing who God is. Don't get me wrong, many a sermon could benefit greatly from a greater dose of relevance! That aside, the true blessing that preaching imparts is the revealing of God. Relevance is good and necessary, but being revelatory is far superior.

Most sermons lack a revealing of God because most preachers don't continually expose their hearts to God's revealing of himself through the process of exegesis. If you have ever felt the weight of God (the meaning of the word *glory*) during the act of preaching, you know the difference between a relevant sermon and a revelatory one! There is truly no comparison nor substitute. God's desire is for the preached word to reveal who he is, so that people can encounter his very person, not simply secondhand musings about his person.

As foreign as this statement may be, I want to argue that exegesis should be first focused on personal transformation rather than public proclamation. Though this next step in our process brings us closer to the act of preaching, it's still quite a way from an actual sermon and should remain in that space for as long as we can stay there. The word of God is acting upon our souls during this step, fully engaging our minds as well as our hearts. We are entering into the conversation that God has been having with his people throughout all time. As such we should seek to listen and marinate in this process as long as we can.

With your preaching date just a short time away, I know all too well the temptation and often felt need to rush through this step. I want to encourage you to resist this and seek to create margin in your life so you can slowly engage in the process of exegesis. Though the byproduct of this process will be biblically sound messages, that's not the goal. The goal is love. That's always been the goal.

The text you are going to preach on is, first and foremost, God's love letter to you. As you read it devotionally, God has begun to move your heart towards him. He has drawn your attention to himself and has invited you into his love for you. This is sacred and beautiful and it's our privilege as his children. As Haddon Robinson says, "we are first God's children before we are his preachers." During these first two steps we are welcomed into our Father's arms with no other goal than to simply bask in his love for us.

Open your heart and mind deeply as God begins to crack open his word to you his child!

Application:

1. The use of commentaries comes in handy during this step. I have found the website www.bestcommentaries.com to be an amazing resource. It lists the top-rated commentaries for every book of the Bible, so no matter what passage you are studying, this website can help you find a great resource. Begin to explore what trusted scholars have said about this passage as they help you exegete the text.

2. Logos Bible software has been an immense gift to me. The speed, ease, and depth of resources available to preachers is remarkable. I was gifted a Logos Library for my 30th birthday, and every year since have slowly expanded the library through various upgrades. I would recommend the slow and steady growth of this digital library because it allows time for you to familiarize yourself with the software as well as time to save up money since it can be a bit costly.

3. It is a good practice to research how trusted preachers and teachers have explained the text. Search their sermon archives and see how they have preached the text. I would encourage this step in exegesis to happen as late as you can so that others' preaching doesn't overly influence/dominate your own study of the text.

CHRIST

In my household the summer of 2017 will forever be the summer of Minions. The latest Minions movie, *Despicable Me 3*, came out during this summer so everyone was going to see it. I wish I could say that a fun trip to the movie theater was my experience that summer. I kind of enjoy a trip to the movie theater during hot summer days. The air conditioning alone is a draw for me, but alas that was not our experience then. Instead of enjoying the Minions on the big screen, these little characters came to occupy every screen we owned, every day of the summer, sometimes several times a day!

Why was this the case, you may be wondering? I have one word and one number that explains it all. The word is MICHAEL and the number is 2, his age. Michael is our third and youngest child, and 2017 was a fun summer (these words are dripping with sarcasm btw). Michael went from being a great eater to a super picky one that summer and it drove us crazy. Keeping our small kids alive is kind of a big deal for my wife and I. This little dude made that goal super challenging to accomplish! He would throw food he used to love, ignore food he used to ask for, and would sometimes pile up the food in one corner of his tray table so as to say "thanks, but no thanks."

The one saving grace during this summer was the Minions movies. Not the new one that was in theaters, or even their latest two movies. He chose to love the first movie of that series. We would play that movie and he would get mesmerized in front of a screen and be lulled into slowly and painfully (for us) eating. It would take a while, and it wasn't always smooth, but it worked!

The main plot of the movie is simply that the Minions are in search for an evil leader to follow. That's kind of the main reason for their existence. The movie is weird and there is a ton going on amidst the great musical score, so it's easy to lose sight of this simple plot. After you strip away their interesting physical appearance, the gibberish and all the slapstick, the movie is simply about their quest to find a heinous leader whose bidding they could follow.

If you ask Michael what the plot of the movie is, he wouldn't be able to tell you because he is two years old. But honestly if you ask an adult about the plot, it might escape them too. There are all these funny and weird moments, the characters are plentiful and all draw a different kind of attention. The New York and London scenes are cool, so one could get caught up in some of those details. There is also a female character who is an evil leader that takes up a good chunk of the movie, so one could easily think the movie is about her. In the end, all of that stuff is simply entertaining fodder because the story is strictly about the Minions finding an evil leader to follow.

Aside from sharing a brief look into my life as a parent, what does this have to do with preaching, or with Christ, the subject of our next step in the DECREASE preaching matrix? The connection is simply that, like the Minions movies, or many other stories for that matter, the main plot of a story can easily be missed. The truth is that the main plot of the story of scripture is often lost on us as readers. We make the Scriptures about so many other secondary or tertiary matters of importance, all the while missing the main point.

Luke 24:13 tells the post-resurrection story of when Jesus reveals himself to his disciples on the road to Emmaus. In this passage Jesus shares with his disciples how Moses and all the prophets speak of him. This text is arguably one of the most important passages of Scripture because in it Jesus gives us the interpretive key to all of Scripture, namely himself. Jesus is the main plot of all Scripture and he is not shy about that truth!

I remember as a teenager being present for an outreach by my church that will forever stick in my mind. The building our church rented was absolutely packed with hundreds of families! They had come to receive a "box of love," as it was called. This box was filled with a frozen turkey, a fully-cooked ham, some form of pie and all the fixings for a full Thanksgiving dinner. These weren't random families that filled the audience that day; rather, they were families we had visited throughout the year in connection to a monthly Saturday outreach to children. Some of these families were people we had visited for years. On that day, there were countless Muslims, Buddhists, and folks that ascribed to a syncretistic belief system called Santeria, very common in the Caribbean. The atmosphere was charged with a crazy energy.

The preacher said many things that day. But one thing I will never forget was the way he described the centrality of Christ. He talked about how it was possible to be a practicing Muslim without ever personally needing the help of the Prophet Mohammed himself, just as long as one had the message he proclaimed. He said the same of Buddha. But Christianity was unique in that one could not practice our faith without Christ himself. He boldly proclaimed that the message of Christianity could not be received and integrated into our lives apart from Christ. It was a bold and powerful statement. On that day I saw many people respond in faith towards Christ because of it.

In the fifth chapter of John's Gospel as he addresses religious leaders, Jesus reveals something quite septic about the human heart. In this moment he corrects them with respect to their motives for engaging Scripture. It's an interesting passage because he reveals their spiritual blindness even though they practiced an intense, faithful engagement with Scripture. It's a scary passage because it reveals that people can diligently read the Scriptures yet miss the point of it all.

Though impossible in real life, imagine staring at the blazing sun and not having to squint your eyes, turn away, or need sunglasses because somehow you aren't able to see what's clearly shining right in front of you. In essence, this is exactly what happened to these religious leaders. Jesus tells them they ultimately missed the focal point of Scripture, which is the revealing of the captivating brilliance of Christ.

Think about that for a second. God's gift of eternal life is only found in his Son the Messiah. All Scripture points to him, yet these religious leaders missed the centrality of Jesus as the main plot of Scripture. They didn't miss this primary point of Scripture because their study habits were poor or lazy; actually, to the contrary, they were incredibly diligent in their engagement with God's word.

It would be way too easy to be judgmental towards these religious leaders and create distance between the state of their hearts and ours, but we would be incorrect to do so. Though they lived in a different culture from ours, their hearts were no different from ours; we, too, have a remarkable ability to miss God, even in the midst of our very pursuit of him. We carry the same theological disease as they did.

In essence, these religious leaders possessed a savior-less spirituality. Though they believed in God and were waiting for the Messiah, their de facto spirituality was devoid of a messiah. They worked really hard to earn God's salvation. As a result of that posture, they approached God from a place of works and not grace. In the end, their confidence rested on their spiritual disciplines, not on a messiah. Jesus was lovingly and directly pointing out their very approach to the Scriptures was skewed and was missing the point entirely.

It's easy to reason we are not like these people, especially if we are professing Christians. But to do so would be to ignore the true nature of our hearts. Our hearts radically resist the power of grace because grace levels us before God, stripping us of any ground we have to stand upon. Our good works are not good enough in light of grace. Our spirituality is not spiritual enough. On our "best" day grace declares that we are utterly helpless without the Savior.

The third step in developing sermons in the DECREASE process is to ask "how is Christ being revealed in this text?" Though super obvious, unfortunately this step is missed all the time in sermon development, and as a consequence, many sermons are not centered on Christ. It's a crazy thing to consider, but it's quite possible and is often the norm for Christians to attend Christian churches where week after week come to hear Christian preachers preach sermons that have very little to do with Christ! We are not much different from these religious leaders after all.

As much as you and I may want to speed ahead to crafting sermons, similar to the first two steps in this process, this third step is still in the realm of encountering God as his child and is in the BEHOLDING stage of our process. Our joy and privilege in approaching the Scriptures is not that we get to preach sermons from them, but that we get to encounter Christ in them. Christ is our Lord, Savior, Redeemer and a Friend of Sinners. Our posture as we open God's word should be to simply meet him.

Despite so much emphasis on being Christ-centered these days, Christ is still missing from many sermons. My contention is that if Christ is missing from our devotional reading of Scripture, then we can't magically expect Christ to be the focal point of our messages.

One of my favorite things to do with my kids has been to read the *Jesus Storybook Bible*. They love it because it's easy to understand, the illustrations are well done and it tells the story of Scripture in a clear way. Most of all, they love how Christ is present through each story. As much as they love it, I can promise you I have loved it even more because it has profoundly touched my heart. Many a night I found myself fighting back tears as I read it to them, not because I was adverse to them seeing me cry, but because if I let myself go I wouldn't be able to make it through the reading.

One of my favorite parts of the *Jesus Storybook Bible* is the very beginning. The author brilliantly explains that the Bible has many heroes and many rules, yet it's ultimately not about any of those heroes or rules. Though we find moral examples and moral failings in the Scriptures, the main point of the Bible is neither of those things. The author beautifully says that each page "echoes his name," every story reveals who Jesus is to us.

One of my favorite preachers as a teenager was Bishop T.D. Jakes. I know he is a controversial figure to many because of his prosperity gospel leanings. But regardless of how you feel about Bishop Jakes, his power as a preacher is undeniable. His cadence, flow, analogies, and his eloquence are quite amazing. Many of his sermons were used of God to transform my heart because of his gift to address the pains of the human soul with grace and clarity. But there is one phrase he uttered that I will never forget for as long as I live. In preaching from the Old Testament, Jakes belted out that "Christ was the concretization of every Old Testament abstraction." That sentence is mesmerizing and packed with such amazing theological dynamite! He went on to say that every sacrifice, every article in the temple, every character points to Christ. Christ is the thread that runs through the entire tapestry of Scripture, from start to finish. Christ is the interpretive key that unlocks the meaning of God's word.

The greatest felt need of the human heart is Christ, and Christ alone. Christ is what people desperately need, even if they fight it, resist it or deny it. Underneath the lusts of our souls is a true longing in every life that will only find its fulfillment in Christ. It sounds simplistic, but that doesn't make it untrue when we say that Christ is the answer to our deepest brokenness. To be clear, we are not talking about the concept of Christ, an abstract idea of Christ, or a historical description of Christ as an archetype for our humanist aspirations. The Christ who is the answer is the Christ that the Apostle Paul says is "the Hope of Glory." Christ, who alone is sinless, who alone is Lord, who alone is Messiah, full of grace and truth, is the answer we are searching for. It is this Christ that we are privileged to proclaim!

In this pre-sermon, BEHOLDING phase of our process, as we meet God in the text of Scripture the question we are asking is two-fold: 1) "how is Christ revealed in this text?" and 2) "how is this properly interpreted in light of Christ?" Though our ultimate goal is to proclaim Christ in our sermons, at this stage we are not asking these questions for that purpose. We are asking these questions for the purpose of worship. We want to respond towards Christ in worship.

Our devotional reading of Scripture, followed by our exegesis of the text, is cemented in our hearts through the revealing of Christ in that text. As our hearts are being awakened to Christ devotionally, and our minds are understanding God's intent in the passage through exegesis, the end of this process is not information but intimacy with Christ. We come to meet Christ in his word, Christ who is the Word.

If our study of Scripture doesn't first lead to intimacy with Christ, then our sermons won't be more than information transfer. Information is helpful and important, but if the foundation of our sermon development process isn't intimacy with Christ then I fear our sermons will only produce people who have a knowledge about God rather than being enticed to truly know Christ. The preacher saturated with intimacy with Christ communicates more than just facts or conceptual knowledge of Christ. As they preach there is a flowing undercurrent that emanates from their soul. Our preaching should be drenched with personal intimacy, an intimacy that evokes worship from the hearts of our hearers. Preaching should stoke the fires of a yearning to personally worship and encounter Christ, not just hear about him from a second-hand source.

In John Stott's commentary on the book of Acts, *The Message of Acts*, he brilliantly outlines the many facets of Christ that the Apostle Peter proclaimed in his first sermon on the day of Pentecost. As a young pastor, I will never forget reading his exposition of this text and how it illuminated the robust proclamation of Christ in Peter's sermon, while simultaneously being convicted in my own preaching of Christ. I was gripped by how anemic, reductionistic and narrow my intimacy with Christ had been in light of Peter's preaching.

Let's take a look at this passage, highlighting the many ways Peter reveals Christ on that day:

Acts 2:14-41

Then Peter stood up with the Eleven, raised his voice and addressed the crowd: "Fellow Jews and all of you who live in Jerusalem, let me explain this to you; listen carefully to what I say. 15 These people are not drunk, as you suppose. It's only nine in the morning! 16 No, this is what was spoken by the prophet Joel: 17 "'In the last days, God says, I will pour out my Spirit on all people. Your sons and daughters will prophesy, your young men will see visions, your old men will dream dreams.18 Even on my servants, both men and women, I will pour out my Spirit in those days, and they will prophesy. 19 I will show wonders in the heavens above and signs on the earth below, blood and fire and billows of smoke. 20 The sun will be turned to darkness and the moon to blood before the coming of the great and glorious day of the Lord. 21 And everyone who calls on the name of the Lord will be saved.' 22 "Fellow Israelites, listen to this: Jesus of Nazareth was a man accredited by God to you by miracles, wonders and signs, which God did among you through him, as you yourselves know. 23 This man was handed over to you by God's deliberate plan and foreknowledge; and you, with the help of wicked men, put him to death by nailing him to the cross. 24 But God raised him from the dead, freeing him from the agony of death, because it was impossible for death to keep its hold on him.25 David said about him: "'I saw the Lord always before me. Because he is at my right hand, I will not be shaken. 26 Therefore my heart is glad and my tongue rejoices; my body also will rest in hope, 27 because you will not abandon me to the realm of the dead, you will not let your holy one see decay. 28 You have made known to me the paths of life; you will fill me with joy in your presence.' 29 "Fellow Israelites, I can tell you confidently that the patriarch David died and was buried, and his tomb is here to this day. 30 But he was a prophet and knew that God had promised him on oath that he would place one of his descendants on his throne. 31 Seeing what was to come, he spoke of the resurrection of the Messiah, that he was not abandoned to the realm of the dead, nor did his body see decay. 32 God has raised this Jesus to life, and we are all witnesses of it.33 Exalted to the right hand of God, he has received from the Father the promised Holy Spirit and has poured out what you now see and hear. 34 For David did not ascend to heaven, and yet he said, "'The Lord said to my Lord: "Sit at my right hand 35 until I make your enemies a footstool for your feet."' 36 "Therefore let all Israel be assured of this: God has made this Jesus, whom you crucified, both Lord and Messiah." 37 When the people heard this, they were cut to the heart and said to Peter and the other apostles, "Brothers, what shall we do?" 38 Peter replied, "Repent and be baptized, every one of you, in the name of Jesus Christ for the forgiveness of your sins. And you will receive the gift of the Holy Spirit. 39 The promise is for you and your children and for all who are far off—for all whom the Lord our God will call." 40 With many other words he warned them; and he pleaded with them, "Save yourselves from this corrupt generation." 41 Those who accepted his message were baptized, and about three thousand were added to their number that day.

Where do we begin? What an amazing proclamation of Christ by the Apostle Peter! Let's look at some of the ways Peter reveals Christ:

● Jesus of Nazareth. Peter is saying here that Christ lived among them, that he came from a specific place.

● Accredited by God to you by miracles. Peter attests to the miraculous ministry of Christ.

● Put him to death by nailing him on the cross. Christ crucified is put forth before the people.

● God raised him from the dead. Christ resurrected is proclaimed.

● Holy one. The distinct holiness and anointedness of Christ is highlighted.

● Resurrection of the Messiah. Christ as promised and awaited Savior, the one who fulfills the prophetic hopes of Israel.

● Nor did his body see decay. This Jesus whom Peter proclaims was fully human, had a body, and his body did not waste away in the tomb. This sermon confronts Gnostic heresies that would eventually surface in the church, dispelling the false idea that Christ was a spirit having the illusion of a physical body.

• Exalted to the right hand of God. Christ not only rose from the dead but he also ascended to the right hand of God. By this act, Christ is held forth as a universal Savior, not a private savior that we can choose.

• Received from the Father the promised Holy Spirit. Christ is the baptizer in the Spirit.

• The Lord said to my Lord. Christ is Lord over all creation, with full authority.

• Both Lord and Messiah. Peter upholds Christ as Lord and Savior, not either/or.

• In the name of Jesus for the forgiveness of sins. Christ is proclaimed as the one who forgives our sin.

I highlight this text to give a broad sampling of how Christ is revealed to us in Scripture, and to challenge us to expect to encounter the fullness of who Jesus is, not a narrow view of him or just the aspects of him that we may be more comfortable.

The fullness of Jesus is what we need to confront the fullness of life and all its complexities. If we examine the deficiencies in our soul, idols that remain unchecked, sin that is not repented of, we will soon discover areas in our lives that lack an encounter with an aspect of who Jesus fully is. The issue most of us face is that we worship a smaller Jesus in our hearts than the big Jesus that is revealed to us in Scripture. A reduced Jesus in our devotional lives will never become an expansive, glorious Jesus in our preaching as we can never boldly proclaim a fuller Jesus than the one we have personally encountered.

As we prepare to preach the word of God, this step brings us closer to the delivery of a sermon. Yet, we are still far from it. Though this step is the pinnacle and penultimate substance of any God-glorifying, life-giving sermon, this step is first and foremost the bedrock of Christian living before it is the substance of a sermon. Encountering Christ in this manner, first and foremost, prepares us to live in the presence of Christ and for Christ before it ever prepares us to preach about Christ. But now having encountered Christ in his word, we are definitely on our way to proclaim him to the world.

Application:

1. How is Christ being revealed to you in this text?

2. How are you being personally challenged and comforted by how Christ is set forth in this text?

3. What aspects of Christ in this text do you find missing from your personal formation as a follower of Jesus?

4. Take time to worship, adore and repent in light of who Christ is in this text. Encounter Christ richly as his child as you prepare to consider how you will preach Christ.

REDEMPTIVE ARC OF SCRIPTURE

Years ago I had the privilege of hearing Andy Crouch lecture on his book *Playing God: Redeeming the Gift of Power.* I can honestly say it was one of the more insightful times of learning that I can remember! Of his many insights, one remains with me to this day: there is a difference between our functional Bible and the actual Bible. I've never read the Bible the same way since!

Crouch shared that, for most Christians, our functional Bible begins in Genesis 3 at the fall of humanity and ends in Revelation 20 at the lake of fire; that is, God's story begins with humanity being broken by sin and ends with the fires of judgment. Though these two moments are truly scriptural and should be pillars in our theological understanding of life, they are far from the complete story of God.

The story of God in Scripture doesn't begin at the fall, nor does it end in judgment. Rather, it begins with creation (Genesis 1) and ends with the renewal of the world (Revelation 22). As we engage the story of God in Scripture, it's important to begin and end the story where God begins and ends it. The difference this has on our personal study of Scripture as well as our preaching of Scripture is nothing short of amazing!

If God's story doesn't begin with the fall of humanity, what impact does this have on our understanding of God and his plan for our lives? For starters, seeing God through the lens of Genesis 1 and 2 before we wrestle with Genesis 3 informs us that God is a creator, and that his creation was created for good and for his good pleasure. The fall of humanity in Genesis 3 and God's response to our sin is so profound and so significant that if we are not careful we can lose sight that God is, first and foremost, a creator, not a judge of humanity's sin. If the story of God begins in Genesis 3, our view of ourselves will not begin with the truth that we are created by God, that we are the objects of his delight, and that he desires for us to flourish. If we start at Genesis 3, we will see ourselves first and foremost as broken sinners; we will lose sight of the primacy of our identity as created beings.

I think there is a real danger in making Genesis 3 the cornerstone of our identity as people. When the fall of humanity is our starting point for how we see ourselves and others, it requires considerable work to try and see people as being created by God and possessors of his image. If the fall of humanity is our starting point, we will likely be slower to see people as fearfully and wonderfully made by God, as possessors of his image, and deserving of dignity and respect, regardless of our shortcomings. Making Genesis 3 our starting point not only lessens our view of people, it also dims our view of the immensity of God's holiness. Without first understanding the beauty for which we were first created, we won't be able to fully grasp the destructiveness of sin and we won't fully appreciate the great cost Christ paid to save us. We lose sight of how dreadful sin truly is.

And we also lose sight of how truly wonderful grace really is.

But for the purposes of this book, one of the dangers of not understanding the narrative arc of Scripture is that it will cause our study of Scripture to lose critically important context. The loss of the meta-narrative of Scripture negatively impacts our ability to fully preach God's word. Every text of Scripture is only understood within its context. We derive the context for each passage by understanding the intent of the author, the historical setting in which the author penned the passage, the grammatical structure and the meaning of the words in the original languages and even the testament (whether Old or New Testament). To unlock the deeper context of Scripture, we must understand both the centrality of Christ in Scripture and that Scripture can only be truly understood in the identity of Christ. But even if we employed each of these key steps in understanding the context of a passage of Scripture, some of the deeper meaning of the text will be lost when we don't understand how the passage fits within the narrative arc of Scripture.

When I refer to the *narrative arc of Scripture* and when you consider the title of this chapter, I'm actually referring to the same thing. The title of this chapter is "The Redemptive Arc of Scripture," which is another way of describing the narrative of arc of Scripture, with some significant teeth.

Hermeneutics is the science or method of interpretation. Whenever we interpret Scripture, there is a method that entails a sound, agreed upon standard that renders the clearest, most unbiased understanding of a passage possible. What I'm proposing is that understanding God's redemptive work and plan as seen in the story of Scripture is a vital key to interpreting Scripture. In other words, the meta-context behind the context of each individual passage is God's redemptive work. Unless we view individual passages in light of this bigger narrative, we will miss critical insights and truths.

I was introduced to this amazing concept by my brothers Ruben Soto and Robert Guerrero through the training programs they lead at Redeemer City to City, the church planting arm of Redeemer Presbyterian Church in New York City. I owe so much to these men, and to the generosity of spirit that exudes from Redeemer and their pastor Dr. Timothy Keller. The incredible training, coaching and support they extend to church planters and pastors alike is such a gift! One caveat: they taught these concepts far better and clearer than perhaps I will. So if I don't do a good job explaining this, it's all my fault. But if I succeed, it's all to their credit.

The Redemptive Arc of Scripture has four movements. These movements are embedded in the narrative arc of Scripture. The four movements are Creation, Fall, Redemption, and Renewal. Understanding these movements of God's story forms a hermeneutic, a way of interpreting the word of God.

As stated earlier in this chapter, the story of God begins in Creation. Humanity and everything we see in this world was originally created for God. Though we see creation marred by sin, it's important to understand that the original state of creation was a state of goodness. Everything in this world (ourselves included) was all created for good, for the enjoyment of God and for the flourishing of the things that were created.

The story of God moves quickly and decisively in Genesis 3 towards what is understood as the Fall of Humanity. In Genesis 3 humanity rebels against God, replacing God at the center of their lives, choosing themselves to be their own gods. Right and wrong would no longer be understood in relation to God and his commands. From that moment we would create our own moral compass. We would determine right from wrong independently from God. The results of this rebellion on the created world have been tragic, to say the least. But the greatest impact of the fall has been felt in our relationship with God. Sin caused humanity to die spiritually, making us unable to walk in unbroken fellowship with God. Ephesians 2:1-3 describes the fall by stating that sin caused us to die spiritually.

Thankfully there is good news! The third movement in the story of God is Redemption. After the fall, we see God's work of redemption set in motion, culminating in the cross of Christ. God did not abandon his creation; rather, he stepped into his creation in order to save it. God became fully human, entering this world as a vulnerable baby. Think about that for a moment. The most powerful being in the universe became a helpless child in order to redeem us!

Christ grew up from childhood into manhood. Along the way he experienced every temptation we have ever faced. Isaiah 53 says that Christ would be "a man of sorrows and acquainted with grief." On the cross he experienced the depths of rejection, physical abuse, emotional isolation and pure torment. Redemption for humanity was drenched in blood on that cross. What a costly redemption! Yet, three days later Christ was raised from the dead, declaring a new day for humanity. The empty tomb proclaims that death, the last enemy, does not have the final word. A new world and humanity is possible through the redemption of Christ.

The plan of God doesn't end with personal salvation but extends to the renewal of all creation. Going back to the training I attended with Andy Crouch, I remember as he shared that the story of God doesn't end in a lake of fire but with a new city coming down from heaven. God would renew his creation! It was pretty earth-shattering for me to consider the implications of this. Up until that point I never considered that God would renew his creation. It was good enough for me to believe that he would renew people, but renewing all of creation was not something I had ever considered. From that day onward the Scriptures have come alive with respect to God's desire to renew all aspects of life, and the hope this truth has instilled in me has been profound. When I walk past housing projects, when I meet families that are steeped in poverty or encounter deeply entrenched racism or injustices in this world, my heart still breaks, but it breaks with hope. God will renew all of creation!

When it comes to understanding a passage of Scripture, it's important that we understand the context of that individual passage. But understanding how it connects to greater story of Scripture unlocks so much richness. God's redemptive power is embedded in the grander story of Scripture. When we see those connections, the individual passage becomes more vivid. In essence, the story of an individual passage or book of the Bible finds its greater meaning within the larger story of God. I have found Zack Eswine's writings incredibly encouraging, especially his book *Preaching to a Post-Everything World*. In this book he speaks about discerning "hints" of creation, the fall, redemption and renewal when we are unpacking a text. I find his approach and insights so helpful in encouraging us to look for the narrative arc of Scripture within specific passages. He explains that not every passage has hints of all four movements of the narrative arc, but that each passage possesses at least one movement of the full story of God.

Connecting the context of a passage with the larger context of the story of God adds weightiness to the text as we apply it to our hearts. Discerning a hint of creation in a passage is amplified when we connect it to God's plan of creation. Embracing what it means to be a fallen creature in a fallen world takes on greater meaning when we connect a passage to the story of the fall. The same weightiness carries when we connect to God's plan of redemption and renewal in Scripture. Incredible grace and impact upon our hearts occurs when we make these connections.

In our discipleship it's quite possible for us to learn passages of Scripture, even entire books of Scripture, and still not connect to the greater narrative of Scripture. What results is a faith that is somewhat disjointed and skewed from God's big picture. If our faith lacks one of these movements it will play out in our lives in significant ways.

For example, if our understanding of God's plan doesn't begin with creation but falsely begins with the fall, then it will be very difficult to see the inherent dignity and worth in people and all of creation despite the brokenness of sin. Even if we are people who care for creation in terms of nature and the planet itself, if we miss the fact that God's story begins in creation, then our care for creation won't be theologically grounded. It might be sincere and heartfelt, but it won't be anchored in God's truth as it should be.

If our understanding of God's plan is rooted in God's work of creation but overlooks the fall, then we are likely to miss the pervasive impact sin has had on all of life. We may find ourselves having an overly romantic view of life and people without the necessary counterbalance. Though creation has intrinsic value, it is still broken by sin. The brokenness of sin should temper how we relate to creation, especially to people. I remember hearing Pete Scazzero from New Life Fellowship in Elmhurst, Queens, once brilliantly say that all of the Bible can be summed up in the expression, "You are deeply loved, but you can't be trusted." If we miss the impact of the fall in our theology, we will err on the side of emphasizing the truth that we are deeply loved, while ignoring the painful but necessary truth that we can't be trusted.

Lacking the anchor of redemption in our understanding of Scripture eliminates our hope for all of creation in the face of the horrors of sin. Without a firm rooting in God's redemption, sin can easily feel too powerful and overwhelming. This would tempt us to lose hope, to lose courage in the work of confronting sin, and ultimately to shy away from proclaiming the power of God's redemptive love. God's work of redemption through the birth, death, burial and resurrection of Christ is the only true hope we have in our broken world. Redemption is possible for all of creation because God has acted in Christ. Regardless of how grim things may seem, our confidence is found in Christ who has the power to redeem us.

As glorious as redemption in Christ is, God's story extends towards the renewal of creation. In Revelation Christ promises that he "makes all things new." The scene in Revelation of a new city coming down from heaven embodies this promise of Christ making all things new. What a promise! All we see that has been marred by sin will not only find redemption in Christ, but it will one day experience complete renewal. The world will not remain bent towards decay; rather, it will be made new in the final work of God. The resurrection is a foretaste of this promise, a first-fruits of what's to come. In light of this future promise, we have present hope as we live as bold witnesses for Christ. Even in the face of the disarray that exists in the world, despair doesn't rule over us because we have a promise from God that this world will be made new again. This promise give us vision beyond our day-to-day grind and responsibilities as we see that God is linking our lives to something bigger, namely the renewal of all of life.

In our DECREASE matrix this step takes place in the BEHOLDING section. While this concept bridges us closer to the act of preaching, we are still only concerned with making sure the truths of God are deeply penetrating our own hearts. Connecting the context of a particular passage to the greater arc of God's story adds tremendous weight to those passages for our own lives. That's our primary concern for now.

That being said, this step is getting closer to the act of preaching. So at this moment it's appropriate to direct our thinking towards how this plays out in preaching. Once you identify the various elements of God's story within a text and have first experienced the power of those truths yourself, preaching those truths becomes quite a joy! Let's walk through a text as an example.

Romans 5:1-11 is a powerful text of Scripture. Let's take a look at this passage:

Romans 5:1 Therefore, since we have been justified through faith, we have peace with God through our Lord Jesus Christ, 2 through whom we have gained access by faith into this grace in which we now stand. And we boast in the hope of the glory of God. 3 Not only so, but we also glory in our sufferings, because we know that suffering produces perseverance; 4 perseverance, character; and character, hope. 5 And hope does not put us to shame, because God's love has been poured out into our hearts through the Holy Spirit, who has been given to us. 6 You see, at just the right time, when we were still powerless, Christ died for the ungodly. 7 Very rarely will anyone die for a righteous person, though for a good person someone might possibly dare to die. 8 But God demonstrates his own love for us in this: While we were still sinners, Christ died for us. 9 Since we have now been justified by his blood, how much more shall we be saved from God's wrath through him! 10 For if, while we were God's enemies, we were reconciled to him through the death of his Son, how much more, having been reconciled, shall we be saved through his life! 11 Not only is this so, but we also boast in God through our Lord Jesus Christ, through whom we have now received reconciliation.

Creation. Though this text doesn't speak of creation directly, the work of God in Christ leading towards our full reconciliation with God can be argued to describe God's creation in reverse. We were made to experience unhindered relationship with God and each other. We were made to experience the love of God in relationship to him.

Fall. This text doesn't hold back any punches while it lovingly and truthfully tells us we are sinners and ungodly. God not only gives us good news he also gives us bad news, and it doesn't get any worse than the truth that we are sinners. The text goes on to call us God's enemies! Did you catch that? Enemies! This speaks to a deeper issue than simply sinning occasionally or committing sins for reasons we can explain and almost excuse. As enemies of God, sinners live in open hostility towards God.

Redemption. Christ's love is vividly demonstrated by his act of dying for us sinners. Dying for good, deserving people is noble, but that would not be as scandalous as dying for someone who has brought pain and suffering to others. Imagine the worst criminal in history, someone who has committed horrendous acts of oppression and injustice. Now imagine someone saintly, someone that is kind and full of promise, dying to save the monstrous person you just imagined.

Renewal. This passage gives us hope that not only our sins are washed by the justifying sacrifice of Christ, it also says that by the power of the Spirit our character can be transformed. Our character can be transformed to the degree that we can now glory in suffering. This change in our souls now allows us to make our boast in the Lord, not in ourselves or anything else. What a change God has wrought! This change in our souls is a sampling of the renewal that God has promised for the world.

You won't find every element of God's story in a text, and sometimes you will only find a hint of it. But every text has at least one element of God's story. Whether it is creation, the fall, redemption or renewal, one of those aspects will be found in the text.

As you are getting closer to preaching, detecting the elements of God's story within the text should play a significant part in shaping the direction and tenor of your message. If God's work of creation is in the text, it would be an utter loss to not focus on creation in your sermon. If the fall is seen in the text, it would be detrimental to not frame the message with that in mind. The same applies for redemption and renewal. Any aspect of God's story in the text should be understood as we seek to apply those truths first to our own lives, but it should also impact the shape of the message.

We are getting closer to preaching! Each step prepares us towards that faithful act. As you continue to sit with the text you are going to preach, allow each step in this process to press God's truths deeper into your heart. May your heart be awakened as you pour over God's word in Devotion. Allow the insights you garnered through Exegesis give you understanding as your mind begins to grasp what your heart has been awakened to by God. In this process, Christ has been revealed to you in this text. You can now see Christ vividly and your heart is resounding in worship towards him. This next step of connecting the context of the passage to the larger context of Scripture is drilling God's word deeper into your soul, but it's also inching you closer to preaching. The Redemptive Arc of Scripture immerses us in the story of God. Not only will the story of the passage you are studying come alive as it connects to God's bigger story, by God's grace, our own personal stories find their meaning within God's larger story. Throughout this process you are being transformed; you are slowly, but surely being prepared to preach the glories of Christ. Let's keep diving in!

Application:

1. Sit with the passage you are studying in light of the Redemptive Arc of Scripture.

2. What elements of the greater story of God do you see in this passage?

3. How is God impressing his word deeper into your heart as a result of the insights you are gaining from this step? How are you experiencing the truths of God's creation, the fall, redemption and renewal?

4. Though this step is not primarily concerned with preaching, it is getting you closer to that act as it shapes the form of your message. What elements of God's story do you see shaping your future sermon?

EVANGELION

The Gospel is often described as the message that brings us to saving faith in Christ, thus relegating the Gospel as strictly good news for the sinner. While this description of the Gospel is valid, the Gospel is just as much for the converted Christian. The Good News not only saves the sinner, but it also grows the saint. The transformative center of our faith is not our efforts at righteousness or our attempts to try harder in obedience. In other words, we are not saved by the Gospel and should then quickly move our efforts towards our own sanctification. Our faith begins in the Gospel, grows from the Gospel, is rooted in the Gospel and should be completely drenched in the Gospel.

Let's look at two passages illustrating this truth. The first passage is in Paul's letter to the Colossians. Colossians 2:6 says, "So then, just as you received Christ Jesus as Lord, continue to live your lives in him, rooted and built up in him, strengthened in the faith as you were taught, and overflowing with thankfulness." This verse tells us the same way we received Christ is the same way we should continue to live our lives in him. The Gospel that starts us on our journey with Christ must be the core of what moves us forward in our walk with God. It isn't simply a doorway into the room of grace, it's the actual room itself.

1 Corinthians 15:1 says: "Now, brothers and sisters, I want to remind you of the Gospel I preached to you, which you received and on which you have taken your stand. By this Gospel you are saved, if you hold firmly to the word I preached to you. Otherwise, you have believed in vain."

Notice this text says the Gospel was preached to the Corinthians. The Gospel is what saved them, but it's also what they are standing on. This verse not only says the Gospel saved them; the Gospel also has ongoing spiritual power in their lives as they hold firm to it. Gospel hope is available for our pre-Christ life, for our present struggles and growth as a Christian, and for the future glory it will reveal.

Often our understanding of the Gospel is a reduction of the Gospel found in Scripture. Recently I heard David Whitehead from Redeemer City to City talk about our tendency as Evangelicals to gravitate towards either the "bloody cross" or the "empty tomb." The bloody cross communicates the severity and ugliness of our sin by recognizing that the death of the perfect Messiah was necessary to redeem us from our sin. The bloody cross also communicates how deeply loved we are by God our creator and redeemer. Christ died for us, not because he had to, but because he wanted to. His love for us was the motive for his death. The bloody cross is Good News.

The empty tomb is also profoundly Good News. Death was not the final word regarding our sin and brokenness. Christ's resurrection is the final word! Where death and despair once reigned, now new life is available to us from Christ. The resurrection declares to people once dead in their sins that we can now live again!

Though the bloody cross and the empty tomb are most certainly good news for the world, thankfully they are not the totality of the good news. The Gospel is so much more. Gloriously more!

Mark 1:14-15 tells us something fascinating from the beginning of Jesus' earthly ministry: "After John was put in prison, Jesus went into Galilee, proclaiming the good news of God. 'The time has come,' he said. 'The kingdom of God has come near. Repent and believe the good news!'" Jesus proclaims the Gospel, the Good News, to the known world. Here is how an incomplete or skewed understanding of the Gospel could obscure this passage. If our understanding of the Gospel is strictly a bloody cross or an empty tomb, this verse becomes incomprehensible because the Good News Christ proclaimed was neither a bloody cross or an empty tomb. We understand from the Gospel accounts (Matthew, Mark, Luke and John) that Jesus didn't speak openly about his death and resurrection to the crowds. He only spoke of these things to his disciples in private and even they didn't understand what he was saying. In the midst of a Roman culture that was marked by death and violence, the proclamation that a messiah would be dying for people was not good news at all. How could the messiah's death free them from Roman rule and oppression? If the bloody cross of Christ wouldn't be received as Gospel to those hearers, and even as spectacular as the resurrection would be, it still would not explain the Good News Jesus preached.

So the question arises, "What was the Good News that Jesus began proclaiming?" The answer is in this passage. Because of our narrow categories of the Gospel we can easily miss it, but the Good News that Jesus preached can be summed up in the name "Emmanuel," which means

"God with us." The good news Jesus proclaimed was that God's Kingdom was at hand, that it was with us through his Incarnation. Before the bloody cross and the empty tomb, the good news is that God entered the world as a crying, vulnerable infant and walked the streets of Jerusalem for us. God almighty would walk among humanity, his feet accruing dust and dirt as he traveled the earth. God among us! Jesus says that because he is among us, this means that the Kingdom of God is at hand, that it is near.

The Good News of the Incarnation is that God is with us. Christ walking with us, being with us, living a fully human life is the Gospel. It's quite a profound Gospel because it means God knows fully what it is to be us. He connects fully with our humanity and now through the Incarnation our humanity can be fully redeemed. That is good news indeed! Every fear, rejection, pain and suffering that hits our lives because we are human beings can be fully redeemed because of the Incarnation.

Think about the implications of this truth for the poor and marginalized of the world. Consider the Good News for the man or woman in prison that is found in the truth that Jesus knows fully what it's like to be human. Imagine what the Incarnation sounds like to people who have experienced racism and abuses from people with power. The Incarnation says God is with us. Even before the God of the universe extends his power to address our ills, his first act of grace is to simply, yet profoundly, be with us. He sits with us in our pain and loneliness. He is near us when we are rejected. Christ understands what it is like to be you and I. This is glorious good news!

The Incarnation also heralds that the Kingdom of God is at hand. God's rule and reign are here. To people who were living in the Roman world, a world where the rule and reign of the Caesars was so pervasively felt, the hope that "God's kingdom is here" was quite profound to those hearers. Jesus was saying the time had come for God's power, reign, and righteous authority to come to bear upon all of life. With the arrival of this kingdom comes the arrival of its King. The world that has been turned upside-down due to sin will now begin to be turned right-side-up because of Christ.

The Good News is the Incarnation, the Bloody Cross and the Empty Tomb. But thankfully it is so much more! In the Christian calendar, these three acts of God are celebrated yearly through Christmas, Good Friday and Resurrection Sunday. During these days, through our various gatherings as the church and even the ongoing receiving of the sacraments of Communion, we are brought into the redemptive drama represented by those days. As much as these holy days proclaim Good News, we would be remiss if our understanding of the Gospel ended there.

In the Christian calendar there is another holiday not celebrated with as much attention as Christmas, Good Friday or Easter. This day is just as much Gospel to the world as those other three days. I'm speaking of

Pentecost Sunday. On this day we celebrate the outpouring of the Holy Spirit. The first disciples were gloriously filled with the Holy Spirit on that day, fulfilling the prophecy of Joel 2 that says the Spirit of God would one day be poured out on all flesh. Gone would be the day when only prophets and kings received the Spirit. Joel's prophecy is so bold because he says that, as a result of the Spirit being poured out, we would see women, slaves and the young become full participants in the work of God. People who were greatly marginalized in that culture would now be given equal status in the Kingdom of God, once the Spirit was poured out.

The Holy Spirit's outpouring is Good News because it is through the Spirit that we are empowered to live obedient lives and emboldened to proclaim the message of Christ. It is through the Spirit that we enjoy the experience of being adopted children of God, full members of God's family despite our rebellious past. Romans 8:15 says that it is by the Spirit that we even know we are the children of God and it is by that same Spirit that we are empowered to call God "Abba Father."

Calling God "Abba Father" is quite profound because in that name is found profound Gospel truth. By that name we are calling God DADDY. God as Abba Father not only communicates that God is Father (which is profound in itself), it also communicates that God is a tender father. As Abba Father we now know God is more than an authority figure; he is a loving, inviting, tender God. These two extremes (authority and affection) usually don't mix. Even when they mix there is typically a skewing towards either authority or affection. Now through the Spirit we know and experience God as Abba Father, the one who perfectly embodies authority and affection. J.I. Packer once wrote "The Christian name for God is father." It is through the Spirit that we come to know God as father, as Abba Father.

Pentecost is part of the Gospel message because it also communicates God's provision for God's people to have an emboldened witness of the Gospel. Through the Spirit we have received gifts that grant us supernatural unction towards the act of preaching the Gospel to our broken world. It is through the Spirit's power in and through us that the Gospel makes any inroads into this world at all.

Ultimately it is not the force of our arguments or the eloquence of our words that draws the human heart to repentance. It is not our will power that raises dead sinners to life. Now that we are alive in Christ, it's not human striving that moves us beyond selfishness and fear to lovingly and boldly declare who Christ is. All of these things and so much more are only empowered through the Holy Spirit. The Good News is that we don't simply become believers in Christ, we become family in Christ. It is the Spirit that seals our hearts towards that end and emboldens us to invite any and all into that same family.

While I've tried to show how the Gospel message found in the Incarnation, the Bloody Cross, the Empty Tomb and Pentecost is significantly fuller than the truncated gospels we often preach, it is bigger still than what I've shared thus far. The Good News of God doesn't end with the Spirit being poured out; it continues on in the creation of the Church. In his book *True Story: A Christianity Worth Believing In,* James Choung brilliantly communicates a fuller Gospel. I highly recommend this book as it has greatly helped me share the Gospel with others as well as equip our church towards that end.

Choung talks about the church being sent together to heal the world through the power of God. But he talks about this not as as ancillary thing, rather he describes it as part of the very same fabric of what we would call the Gospel. The fuller Good News is not just all the elements we have been talking about and ending there. Becoming part of the church and being sent out into the world is part of the Gospel. James argues that when we don't include this truth in our Gospel understanding the result is a lack of mission in the world because we stop the Gospel from reaching beyond our own professions of faith. The Gospel becomes trapped in our personal lives when we don't see how being part of the church on mission in this world is just as much a part of the Gospel message.

The very creation of God's church is Good News because when we fully live out our calling as God's people we embody hope for a broken and divided world. God's church is a miracle of his design alone because in it natural-born enemies now become family. In Romans and Ephesians the Apostle Paul teaches that now in Christ the former divisions and hostilities are done away as God in Christ has created a new humanity. According to 2 Corinthians 15, as members of the church we are now reconciled to God and to one another and have been given the ministry of reconciliation. Through our reconciled love and unity, the church proclaims a profound Gospel message to the world, namely that the divisions caused by sin no longer need to divide us if we turn to Christ in repentance and faith. In a world that is torn apart by racism, violence, war and all kinds of schisms, the Gospel message found within the creation of the church is quite profound and deeply needed.

Hopefully these thoughts expand our view of the Gospel, pushing us past the limitations of a narrow and truncated Gospel. When our Gospel understanding enlarges, we position our lives to receive more of God's power in and through us. A fuller Gospel understanding translates into a fuller preaching of the Gospel. What I hope to offer in this chapter is a broader view of the Gospel, a Gospel big enough to grapple with all of life, and a Gospel big enough for all the brokenness in our world. Before all of that takes place though, we need the Gospel to transform our personal lives.

If you are like me, the word EVANGELION is not in your normal vocabulary because your native language is not classical Greek. Despite that disadvantage, I have good news! The word EVANGELION means just that: GOOD NEWS. Evangelion is the Greek word for Gospel.

With this word we have come to the final step in our BEHOLDING section. Though each step in this process is important and builds on each other, this step carries a weight of importance that is hard to convey. Despite my best efforts in this chapter, I have resigned within myself that I will fall short of capturing the full beauty of this word. But the good news is that even an approximation of this glorious concept will have powerful implications for our souls and ultimately our preaching!

Romans 1:16 says "For I am not ashamed of the Gospel, because it is the power of God that brings salvation to everyone who believes: first to the Jew, then to the Gentile." The Gospel is not *a* power of God, it is THE power of God that brings salvation. God's good news in Christ changes everything! The world desperately needs the power that is within the Gospel. As simple as this idea of Good News is, it turns out we in the Christian community have struggled to grasp its simplicity and breadth. The results of this misunderstanding are actually quite detrimental. A mini-gospel or a half-gospel provide only partial Good News to people and a world that needs all the good news we can get.

As helpful as I hope these words have been for your life in general, the purpose of me sharing them in this chapter is to discuss the importance of the Gospel with respect to preaching. Having spent considerable time addressing how we can experience the Gospel personally, now let's address how the Gospel should inform our preaching.

With the text of Scripture before you, here is how the step of Evangelion works. Having read the text through the previous steps in our matrix, this next step asks, "What is the Good News I see in this text?"

One of our aims as we read Scripture should be to press beyond merely gaining religious knowledge. We should seek to continue to behold God in his word until we see and experience the Gospel in our text. Our reading of Scripture should first impart good news to our souls before we could ever proclaim good news to others. I can't stress the importance of this point enough for the sake of preaching of the Gospel. If our reading of Scripture doesn't focus on the Gospel, the likelihood that our preaching will proclaim the Gospel is pretty slim.

Preaching the Gospel begins first with us experiencing the Gospel. That first takes place as we behold the word of God for our own pleasure and delight. Once we have tasted and seen that the Lord is good, then and only then are we in a position to proclaim that goodness to others.

One of the greatest needs in my life as a husband, father and pastor is experiencing the Gospel on a deeper level than my preaching of it. If my preaching of the Gospel outpaces my experience of the Gospel, I run the risk of doing violence to my own soul because I will find myself "selling" a Gospel that I haven't thoroughly savored myself.

As I get older, I find myself observing the steady retreat of my hairline. It's sad. I always knew it was coming based on my family history, but it's sad nonetheless. I remember as a kid watching the commercials for Hair Club for Men. Despite how upbeat those men were about their "new" hair, it always felt sad to watch. Though their hairlines were restored, it doesn't change that they are still aging. As positive of a feeling full hair can give a man, it can't cover up the gaps in our identity that comes with being men in a broken world. That's deep right? That's a lot of words to talk about hair loss right? Well now you know how I'm preaching the Gospel to myself when I stare at my hairline. But I digress.

I reference those commercials because I will never forget the catchphrase. Towards the end of the commercial the spokesperson talking about this amazing hairline restoration procedure says some pretty remarkable words: "I'm not only the president, I'm also a client." Boom! Mic drop! We leave that commercial with the realization that the person describing this product is not merely selling it because it's good for their business. This is not a random product and they are not just a peddler of this good; they have personally experienced it, are thrilled by its results and now they are willing to put out this embarrassing commercial to tell you about their experience of it. (In fairness, they probably didn't think it was embarrassing, but they should have. Just kidding.) That one line added a level of credibility that can't be overstated. They were describing something they believed in because they had experienced it personally.

When it comes to preaching, experiencing the Gospel in a deep, enduring, continuous, firsthand manner is of the utmost importance. It softens my heart and leads me to repentance. In the Gospel I'm cradled in the love of God as his child before I'm sent forth as his herald. With that said, it's important to be clear that a soul that has experienced the Gospel is a soul that must preach the Gospel. It's not a matter of "if" they will preach the Gospel, it is only a matter of when, where, how and to whom they will preach. Have you noticed that one of the fundamental attributes of all people is the tendency to share our experiences with others. We can't help it. Every human being is an evangelist, the only question is what and for whom are you evangelizing.

I always chuckle when people taste something they don't like. Perhaps it tastes sour, is too spicy or maybe even bland. The faces we make when this happen are priceless and crack me up. But what I always wait for is how people tend to offer a sampling of the same food that just disgusted them. It's pretty funny! They took a bite, their face is grimacing and they look over the table at you and say, "This is disgusting, so nasty, HERE TRY THIS!" It's such a weird moment because on the one hand they are sharing and that's nice and should be commended, but on the other hand they are sharing something that's horrible. It's hard to commit to a reaction at that moment. Should I be grateful by their generosity or horrified this generosity is nothing more than an attempt to find company in their misery? This mystery may never be solved!

Whatever the motive, it is clear we are wired to share what we have experienced, regardless if those experiences are good or bad. Because of this human dynamic I'm convinced the severe dearth of Christians actively preaching the Gospel stems from the reality that we have not experienced the Gospel ourselves. The sharing of the Gospel may be sloppy, awkward, rushed and even too intense at times for the hearers with whom we share, but if we have experienced the Gospel, we know it can't be kept to ourselves. We have to share it.

Having experienced the Gospel ourselves, and having spent time beholding the goodness of God in Christ after all these steps, we are now ready to begin to look up from the Scriptures and consider how we will preach the Gospel to others. This is exciting! Our hearts should be pumping, our souls should be stirred and our spirit lifted with joy as we are close to telling others about this glorious Gospel.

A friend of mine, Richard Villodas, Pastor of New Life Fellowship in Elmhurst, Queens, once shared an insight on this matter that I carry with me to this day. He has been one of the most generous men I know when it comes to sharing resources and insights about life, ministry and preaching. He shared that, often in preaching, we rush to application without spending enough time in proclamation. Man, my mind was blown with that statement! He went on to explain that one of the fundamental jobs of preaching is to proclaim what God has done, to extol that, to adore that and gather everyone to behold that. After we have done that, and only after we have done that are we ready to talk about application.

From this insight I have gleaned that, before we talk about what WE MUST DO, we must first proclaim what CHRIST HAS DONE. The starting point of our obedience and our response to God is *his* finished work. The words "it is finished" declared by Christ on the cross are like the pistol that's fired at Olympic track meets. Like those runners who can't start running until that gun is fired, our life in Christ and our ministry for him doesn't begin until we have firmly understood his eternally completed work.

Jonathan Dodson in his book *The Unbelievable Gospel: Say Something Worth Believing* gives us valuable insights as we prepare to preach the Gospel. I highly recommend this book for Christians who want their heart stirred for evangelism, but I strongly recommend this book for preachers. He describes the human heart as seeking acceptance, hope, tolerance and approval. He masterfully shows how the Scriptural metaphors for the Gospel powerfully answer these deep human needs. Dodson demonstrates that we find acceptance in God through the justification from sin that Christ offers. We find hope through the new life that the resurrection of Christ and the regenerating power of the Spirit offers to us. The tolerance we need is found in the redemption that we find in Christ, and the approval we long for is discovered in God's work to receive us as adopted sons and daughters. I highly recommend this book! I'm not doing it any justice by this brief mention. Go and buy it.

As you prepare to preach, a helpful question to ask based off of Dodson's book is:"What Gospel metaphor captures the Good News in this passage?" Pinpointing the Gospel metaphor in the text you are about to preach helps sharpen your focus. It gives you a clearer pathway for preaching and it also helps to peg your preaching to the core, established doctrines of Scripture.

One of the goals of biblically sound, Gospel-centered preaching should be to model a sound handling of God's word to God's people. By modeling how our souls came alive through the text, how we exegete the text, how Christ is seen in that text, how that text connects to the greater story of Scripture, and how that text proclaims the Gospel, God's people are walking away with tools for their own engagement with Scripture. Our desire as preachers should be that people walk away from our sermons less impressed with us and more eager to crack open the word of God themselves. When we focus our sermons on the Gospel, our prayer is that people will overwhelmingly leave saying, "my my, that was Good News" rather than saying "my my, that's a good preacher."

One of the joys of pinpointing the Gospel in a text is that our preaching will now focus on what Christ has done before we ever talk about what we must do. This kind of preaching places the emphasis on who Jesus is and what he has done. It rightly identifies who has done the heavy lifting and properly frames our response. Though we are called to respond to the Gospel in repentance and faith (Mark 1:14-15), we must be clear that repentance and faith is a response to a finished work. We are not accepted, justified, or made new by Christ because our repentance and faith has somehow merited them. What Christ has done has paved the way for all of this and our repentance and faith simply helps us to receive this.

If you have ever preached while feeling an unhelpful pressure or a weight on your soul then you know firsthand the huge benefit of preaching from a "light place." Perhaps the pressure was induced by a need to perform or perhaps the weightiness was due to a burden to genuinely see people transformed as you considered their brokenness. Understanding the Gospel frees us from these burdens because, as we preach, we rightly understand that the hope for transformation doesn't rest on us. The Gospel helps us to know that the life change we yearn for people to experience doesn't rest on our performance or presentation. God's power is delivered to our hearts through the Gospel. This is not to say that a sloppy presentation of the Gospel should suffice because God's power is what gets the job done. In fact, the beauty of the Gospel should compel us to want to communicate it beautifully, but at the same time, it frees us to know that the power of the Gospel rests on God himself, not on our words.

Having clarity on the Gospel in your text also frees us from the ever-present temptation to favor style over substance. The culture surrounding preaching these days has created a strange phenomenon known as "celebrity pastors." That's a strange concept indeed! Who would have ever thought that shepherds would have celebrity status? The shepherds of Jesus' day are turning in their graves over the missed opportunity for them to build a platform, a brand, amass followers, etc. Such a loss! (I'm totally joking, just in case my sarcasm isn't apparent.) Imagine what John the Baptist feels about the lost opportunity to have a large fan base!

Before I sound like I'm totally against celebrity preachers, please allow me to clarify one important thing. In our society that drools over all things that are famous, I love that there are many preachers who have become household names. It is a good thing that there are people known by the public at large through their preaching and teaching of God's word. When those people are searching for answers and longing for hope from God's word, how tragic would it be if they didn't have a starting point for that journey? Thankfully they can go and buy a book or hear a sermon from a well-known pastor. Thankfully many of these well-known preachers preach the Gospel in its fullness, preaching both the good news and the bad news contained in its message. For the sake of those searching for answers, I rejoice that there are good preachers known to the public. The negative I mourn over is that, in our culture, it's possible to become a celebrity for bad reasons. In like manner it's possible to become a celebrity preacher if you're simply an engaging communicator. Our culture prefers soundbites over substance. As a result it's possible to amass a following even if your message has no weight to it.

As people, we are captivated by the power of story. If you doubt that, take for example that Steve Jobs made the majority of his wealth not from Apple, but from his investment in Pixar. The animated stories they told captivated generations of people who in turn paid large sums of money in merchandise. Another example are comedians. Consider the large sums of money people pay to watch their shows or see their specials on television. These comedians hold audiences captive through their gift of telling stories, or telling hard truths through their humorous anecdotes. Preachers can have the same impact on people if they are engaging, regardless if their sermons are void of Gospel truth.

Another factor that can help make a pastor into a celebrity is if they avoid hard truths. People will love you if you make them feel good and never challenge them. It's been said that if you want to make people feel good, sell ice cream, don't become a leader. Sadly many preachers choose the path of preaching solely "ice cream" messages. To be clear, I don't believe we need to be unnecessarily harsh or needlessly offensive in the name of being "prophetic." Many people have been offended by a harsh tone or the way we deliver our messages and that's unfortunate and should be repented of. What we should not avoid is people being offended by the Gospel itself. If we truthfully preach the Gospel, people will be offended. If everyone loves us, that's a clear sign of a problem.

Being clear on the elements of the Gospel helps to free us from these temptations and pitfalls. Gospel clarity softens our hearts with God's love, paving the way for us to preach boldly. The Gospel puts steel in our spines, helping us to withstand the criticisms leveled at us, while also keeping the praises of people from drowning us with vain affirmations.

There is so much more that can be said about the Gospel. My hope is that I've said enough on this point that you can't wait to get with God and his word and hear the Gospel proclaimed to your soul! For every fear, struggle, and opportunity we face, the Gospel has a word for us. As you sit with a text of Scripture in preparation to preach, may you hear the good news ring loudly. May it produce excitement and anticipation for the soon-to-be-moment when you proclaim the good news that has been first proclaimed to you.

Application:

1. Sit with the passage you are studying in light of the Gospel.

2. What elements of the Gospel do you see in this passage?

3. How is God impressing the Gospel deeper into your heart as a result of the insights you are gaining from this step? How are you experiencing the truths of the Gospel?

4. Is there any fear, reluctance or even cowardice that you need to repent of in light of the boldness the Gospel imparts to us?

5. Is there humility, softness, and compassion the Gospel is impressing on you?

6. This step is the last step in the BEHOLD stage of engaging with Scripture. Though the goal is still to receive from God as his child, we are so close to preaching that it's appropriate to begin exploring how this will shape your message. As you consider this step, what elements of the Gospel do you see shaping your future sermon?

PROCLAIMING

Our focus will now shift from BEHOLDING to PROCLAIMING. Having spent ample time beholding the glory of God in Christ our souls have received so much from the Father. We have focused on meeting God first as his children before we consider what it means to preach. We are now reading to begin thinking about the holy task of preaching. At this point our hearts are so full that, as we approach the pulpit, we are approaching it with a word from God that has been deposited deeply in our souls. We are not dragging ourselves to preach reluctantly; we are willingly and passionately anticipating the joy and humble honor of preaching God's word.

Having said that, let's dive into to some important final steps that prepare us to preach.

BEHOLDING

DEVOTIONALLY

How is God awakening your heart through his word?

EXEGESIS

What is the context of this passage?

CHRIST

How is this text understood in light of Christ?

REDEMPTIVE-ARC

How does this text fit within the meta-narrative of Scripture?

EVANGELION

How is the Gospel declared in this text? How do we interpret this text in light of the Gospel?

PROCLAIMING

AUDIENCE

What are the idols in peoples hearts that would resist the Gospel of Christ?

STORY

How will your sermon outline tell the story of God?

EXPECTATIONS

What does God expect people to do based on this sermon? What is your divine expectation as a preacher for this sermon?

AUDIENCE

One of the key, indispensable rules of public speaking is to "know your audience." This rule applies to the fields of marketing, advertising and sales as well. Knowing your audience enhances the impact of your message as it increases the chances that it will be understood and well received. The effective use of this principle can determine whether or not your plans to grow your business, make a sale, influence students, or get your kid to go to bed will actually happen or if your hopes will be dashed.

As vital as this principle is, it also has a shadow side. If you perfect the craft of knowing your audience, it's quite possible that you can become so good at influencing people that you can become nothing more than just a salesperson. Nothing wrong with selling inherently, but when selling something becomes more important than the people you are interacting with, then we have a problem.

When it comes to preaching, our primary motivation in "knowing our audience" should not be to enhance our ability to persuade people towards some end. Rather, it should be to love them. We want to know them so our sharing would be done in a spirit of love. By knowing them from a posture of love, we can be protected from viewing people as projects. We can see them as people made in the image of God who are deeply loved by God.

With the goal of loving people, we want to know our audience because we want to become aware of the idols in their hearts that would cause them to resist the Good News of Christ. With each step in this matrix you have moved closer to preaching. All of these steps will eventually bring you before a gathered people, whether it's a youth group, a Bible study in someone's home or in a coffee shop, a Sunday worship gathering or a large conference hall. The one commonality is that you will be speaking to people. Specifically, you will be speaking to people who, though they are in desperate need of the grace of God, the presence and influence of sin will cause them to resist the Good News.

Consider that for a moment. The human heart is riddled with brokenness that desperately needs healing from God, but it's that same brokenness that resists God's grace. This may sound intense, but preaching is an act of war! Preaching is aimed at the hearts of people, hearts that are the focus of a spiritual battle between the Kingdom of God and the Kingdom of Darkness. I realize for some people the idea of a spiritual battle is outside of your comfort zone. It feels way too primitive for our modern sensibilities. But whatever anthropological/sociological term may feel more comfortable, our modern categories have yet to explain the spiritual condition of our hearts better than Scripture. The Scriptures tell us there is a war raging for the hearts and minds of people, and preaching steps right into the battle zone.

We can't fully love people if we don't truly know them. But to know people is to realize quickly that our hearts are filled with idols. Biblically speaking, the sin of idolatry is one of the most pernicious sins of all. Idolatry is the act of replacing God with someone or something else and choosing to worship that thing. It happens when we consider lesser things as ultimate things and in the process reduce God to a lesser thing. Idolatry is not solely a cognitive choice of placing something else in the place that only God rightly deserves. Rather, it involves our affections and love becoming captive to things other than God. John Calvin famously wrote, "The human heart is an idol factory" in describing our tendency to constantly put things before God.

Through my time with the folks at Redeemer City to City, I have been challenged by their teaching on idols, specifically how idols often hide behind our desires for power, control, comfort and approval. In and of themselves our desires for these four things are not sinful, but they quickly become sinful when they lead us to make good things into ultimate things. These insights have caused me to ask the question, "What is the sin beneath the sin?" in order to discern the roots of idolatry at work in my life.

Your audiences will be full of wonderful people, made in the image of God. I'm sure they are perfectly lovely folks, but nonetheless they suffer from the plague of idolatry. Growing up in poverty, in a single-parent home during the height of the crack-cocaine epidemic of the 80's and 90's, I have seen what brokenness looks like on a street corner. I've seen the wreckage that drug addiction and criminal activity can cause to individuals and communities. For most of my life I have been more familiar with people being broken by failure and despair, but over the last few years I have become increasingly aware that people are just as much broken by success.

I've come to realize that corporate boardrooms can conjure up ways that can create as much human misery as drug dealers. That may sound harsh, but ask the folks who suffered at the hands of the Enron scandal whether they would agree with that statement. The point is not that businesses are bad and the streets are good, but simply that it's easier to overly define brokenness through the things associated with poverty while overlooking sins that are closely related to wealth, power and comfort. Everyone and everything is broken. Where human brokenness persists and wrecks lives, you can be sure an idol is at the core.

Identifying the idols in the hearts of your hearers is a key step in helping to shape your message so those idols are confronted. We don't want to identify those idols so that we know what to stay away from in our preaching. Rather, we want to name them so the light of God's grace and glory can shine on them and expose them for what they really are.

All this sounds great theoretically, until we come face-to-face with the nitty gritty of what this entails. You and I can't name idols in people's hearts and shape messages to confront them in a relational vacuum. Knowing our audience is not authentically done unless you actually spend time with your hearers. If these people are in your church, youth group, college ministry, etc., that means that you must spend time with them.

Now it's important to clarify: if we are spending time with people in order to conduct sermon research, then we are missing the heart of the matter. We discern people's idols through the grid of authentic relationships. Hearing and understanding people's hopes and dreams comes with this territory. Walking with people through pain and struggle is a huge part of knowing your audience and as a result of this we come to discover their idols. Our goal is not to confront the idols of theoretical people. We are not looking to locate people along some conceptual spectrum of idolatry as if this is detached from real life, from true pain and suffering. We are talking about real people held captive to real idols, idols that keep them from experiencing a flourishing life with God.

I remember John Thomas, the Director of Global Training for Redeemer City to City, described preaching that confronts idols in the most compelling way. He shared a personal experience of being at a worship gathering during which the pastor was talking about idols and he felt as if his heart was being exposed. He described the palms of his hands getting sweaty as the pastor preached. He felt shock and horror as the affections of his heart were being exposed, realizing he was a prisoner to those idols. Realizing that his soul truly worshipped something other than Jesus was painful, but the pain paled in comparison to the fear he felt at the idea of living without this idol. It was bad enough for the true state of his soul to be revealed, but now that light was shining on his idol, conceiving of a life without it was terrifying. For good or bad (and clearly idolatry is bad) his life had come to rest on these idols just like ours often do. To repent of our idols confronts our fundamental makeup as people. So if turning away from them isn't freaking you out even a tiny bit, chances are your idols may still be lying dormant in your soul, operating in the background.

Confronting idols to this degree doesn't happen without truly knowing people and loving them. To accomplish this we must "sit where people sit." Which brings us to one of my favorite passages in the Book of Ezekiel. Ezekiel chapter 3, beginning in verse 12 says: "Then the Spirit lifted me up, and I heard behind me a loud rumbling sound as the glory of the Lord rose from the place where it was standing. It was the sound of the wings of the living creatures brushing against each other and the sound of the wheels beside them, a loud rumbling sound. The Spirit then lifted me up and took me away, and I went in bitterness and in the anger of my spirit, with the strong hand of the Lord on me. I came to the exiles who lived at Tel Aviv near the Kebar River. And there, where they were living, I sat among them for seven days—deeply distressed."

As someone who came to Christ in a Charismatic church, the words in the passage are not figurative or allegorical for me. I have sensed the "Spirit lift me" as Ezekiel describes it. I have experienced the "strong hand of the Lord on me." Over the years I have had such sweet encounters with the Lord, and the impact of those encounters has left a deep hunger in my soul for the presence of God. Beyond my personal devotional life, when it comes to preaching I have come to the conviction that all ministry is futile without God's presence and power at work. Preaching that is not drenched in a prayerful longing for God's reality to break through the stubbornness of the human heart won't count for much.

That being said, what grips me in this passage is the simple, yet profound phrase that is the key to developing sermons that will actually confront idols. Without this missing link we won't have clarity on the exact location in people's souls that we need the power of God's presence to break through. Verse 15 says: "I came to the exiles who lived at Tel Aviv near the Kebar River. And there, where they were living, I sat among them for seven days—deeply distressed." The missing step in the development of most sermons is simply to sit "among them." What profoundly prepares us to stand and preach is to first sit with people and listen.

John Maxwell has said, "People don't care how much you know, until they know how much you care." This is generally true, but when it comes to preaching it's intensely true! People can tell the difference between someone who has true empathy for their struggles versus someone who is simply paying lip service to their pain. As preachers we are often strictly concerned with the truth of our messages, while not paying enough attention to the state of our hearts as messengers.

I know this statement will sound extreme, but Ezekiel 3 reminds me that being anointed, sensing the Spirit's power and carrying a burden from God are not enough. If you were raised in a Charismatic church like me, those words are offensive. How could being anointed not be enough? What I've come to realize is that without a true sense of compassion and empathy for the people, I become a bottleneck of sorts, frustrating God's anointing and Spirit from moving through me. I have personally experienced the dynamic of sensing God's presence, of drenching my soul in prayer, and having a burden from God only to have my sermon fall flat. In retrospect, it wasn't a lack of study or even prayer that was the problem, it was a lack of empathy.

Acts 17 is an incredible case study in knowing one's audience. From verses 16 to 34, we read the account of Paul in the city of Athens. The text tells us that day-by-day Paul witnessed to the Good News of Jesus and his resurrection in both the synagogue and the marketplace. At the synagogue he would speak to God-fearing Greeks and Jews. At the marketplace he would have the chance to interact with anyone and everyone in the city. From this daily rhythm of interacting with different people and in different settings, people began to react to his words. He also interacts with Epicurean and Stoic philosophers in the city, a pretty significant thing considering that Athens was such an important center for Greek thought. These verses tell us that some people mocked and called Paul a "babbler" and others said that he was trying to advocate "foreign gods." After all this criss-crossing between the synagogue and the marketplace, we see the people bringing Paul to a place called the Areopagus, where the Athenian court was located. From here the most solemn questions connected with religion were deliberated upon. In fact the Areopagus was the place where Socrates was tried and condemned. The Areopagus is where Athenians and foreigners alike spent all their time talking about and listening to the latest ideas. They bring Paul there because they want to know about the teaching that he is spreading.

During his talk at the Areopagus we find incredible insights with respect to preaching the Gospel in a way that confronts people's idols. One thing is that Paul has taken the time to deeply understand the people of Athens. He has considered their architecture, the way they do business, their religious and philosophical centers and leaders. Paul says that during one of his undoubtedly many walks throughout the city he noticed all of the idols in the city and his spirit was vexed. Imagine an entire city built around the worship of false gods! In particular, he noticed an altar during his walk around Athens that had an inscription "to the unknown god." As he spoke at the Areopagus, he affirms his hearers are clearly a religious people, but at the same time he confronts the ignorance in their religion as seen by their worship of a god that was unknown to them. Brilliantly he uses this identifiable gap of knowledge in their worship and worldview as an entry way for him to preach the Gospel.

During his sermon we find that Paul went to great lengths to know his audience. He quotes one of their poets, which tells us he took the time to engage with the artistic and creative class in that city. Artistic expression is one of the ways people express their deepest longings, communicating their hopes and dreams and their desire for transcendence. Paul took the time to truly know these people.

The true brilliance of this moment is how he allowed all of this to dramatically shape his presentation of the Gospel. Quite differently from other sermons of Paul in Acts, he doesn't begin his sermon with Abraham or other patriarchs of the faith. He doesn't mention messianic prophecies or even talk about the sacrificial death of Christ on the cross. He frames his message around creation and how within creation we discover a longing and searching for God by all people, regardless of where they come from or the era of history they live in. How appropriate of him to connect the search for God in the Athenians with the search for God by all people everywhere and all times. From that starting point Paul connects their experience as created beings who are searching for God with the resurrection of Jesus. What's interesting is that his resurrection is not described in terms of justifying sinners, rather it is described in terms of Jesus having the authority to judge and weigh the substance of our lives. Paul was arguing that one day we would have to give an account for the thoughts we think and the lives we live. Standing in a place where judgments were declared by people in authority, establishing Jesus as Judge makes complete sense.

These words must have hit home with a people who sat around all day talking and thinking about the latest ideas. Paul was unearthing the connection between their daily lives with a much deeper longing for transcendence and meaning. He pointed out there was a much a bigger purpose in our lives than what they were aware of, showing them how their search for God was leading them to Christ (whether they realized it or not) -- Christ whose resurrection uniquely qualifies him to judge our lives.

In speaking of the resurrection, it's important to note how jarring this must have been. Up until this point we see Paul taking the time to know them deeply. This intimate knowledge of their culture afforded him the wisdom to shape his message in a way they would understand. In essence, his knowledge of his audience allowed him to connect deeply with them. His listeners knew that Paul cared, that he took the time to listen to them and understand them. If that's where Paul ended that would have been amazing in itself, but that's not where he stopped. His goal was not simply to know them so his preaching could connect with them; he ultimately loved them enough that he wanted to confront their idols.

His goal was to preach the Gospel to them, and he knew the Gospel would offend them. By taking the time to deeply connect with them, Paul eliminated the possibility of needlessly offending them by cultural insensitivity or being emotionally aloof to their lives. This is important to understand because often people are not offended by the Gospel, rather they are offended by our insensitivity and ignorance of their lives and culture. He took the time to know them well enough so the offense would be a result of hearing the Gospel, not his approach to sharing the Gospel. Ultimately, if the Gospel is what offends, then people we can live with that. When Good News offends people we know their idols are being confronted, and if we love them, then we can withstand their anger.

Knowing our audience and the idols that enslave their lives empowers us to speak the truth in love. We must bring the weight of God's truth to bear on the idols that keep people bound. The painful truth is that idolatry is a sin, a sin that is deeply offensive to God. That has to be confronted. Idolatry promises so much, yet delivers so little, therefore the hollowness of idolatry must be revealed. That is jarring, to say the least. People need to hear the truth about this, but it must be done in love. We must love people so much that we are willing to slowly and deeply get to know them. Their dreams and hopes should move our hearts to tears as we consider how unfulfilled they will remain if they continue to worship idols. Knowing our audience should lead us to love people - people who need to hear difficult truths but who should receive them from messengers that are drenched in compassion and empathy.

Hopefully your heart is stirred at this point and you are asking "How can I better know people so that I can effectively preach the Gospel to them?" The greatest answer to this question is found in the Incarnation itself. As Christ became fully human in order to dwell in our world, so must we embrace our humanity and the humanity of others through intentional relationships. Prayerfully walking our neighborhoods and cities should be a regular rhythm for us. Identifying the religious, business and cultural centers in your community is an absolute must. Once identified, we should seek to build relational trust where people would feel comfortable inviting us closer. The right to preach to others is a right we slowly earn with people who are on the outside looking in. This slow process builds our credibility before people's eyes, but it also changes us in the process. Nothing will make us want to pray for people more, and love and serve them, quite like taking the time to know them and allowing our hearts to be pierced by their brokenness and the hollowness of their idolatry. We won't remain the same if we truly engage with people. The change we experience will better equip us to love people well as we confront their idols.

The process I just described is similar, but looks slightly different when it comes to Christians. As Christians, though we profess to worship Christ as Lord, we are just as idolatrous as the people of Athens. Our idolatries often surface when it comes to things like the worship styles we prefer, the theological frameworks we prefer, and our church traditions. As important as these things are, we often elevate them to a status that is only fitting for God himself. Another way the idols of Christians surface is through pastoral conversations. During seasons of struggle, at the heart of those struggles is often a wrestling with idols. Their insufficiency is being revealed, yet our hearts still want to cling to them at all costs. As a pastor I am learning to listen deeply to what people share with me in order to understand what is robbing their affections from Jesus. It's hard work and I'm constantly confronted with how much I need to grow in this area, but I'm convinced I need to learn to do this really well. As someone who is about to preach, so should you.

As you prepare to put some shape and structure to your message, do so with your audience in mind. Take into account recent conversations you have had with people in your audience. Recall interactions you have had with neighbors in your community. Consider the ethnic makeup of your audience and how their unique cultural histories cause them to be the people they are. Reflect on the pace of life in your city and the challenges/ opportunities this causes in our lives. Think about how a young, old, single, married, divorced person would hear and understand what you are about to say. Seek to understand how skeptics and people that are antagonistic to the faith would interpret your message.

This is hard, intentional work, but without it we won't be equipped to pray and preach with focus. This exercise should lead us to pray for people as we identify the idols that hold them captive. As we uncover their inner objections to the Gospel, this should drive us to pray hard, yearning to see their eyes opened to the truth of God's love. This work should also influence how we shape our message. Understanding people on this deep of a level enables us to eliminate needless offenses to our message so that the Gospel can be heard clearly. If the Gospel offends people, we can't help that, but we can work hard to not offend people with careless and insensitive communication.

Though we have been focusing our attention on knowing our hearers, it's important to consider how the broader context of culture shapes those very people. Depending on where you live, the degree of secularization, post-Christian worldviews and anti-Christian sentiments will vary. But at the end of the day, we are all being impacted by these large cultural shifts. The broader culture and our Christian faith have diverged significantly over the last several decades. For the sake of effective preaching, we must wrestle with these realities.

The following are some reflective questions and steps I try to consider during this stage of my sermon prep:

- As I begin to craft my sermon with a particular audience in mind, am I choosing to speak in a manner that will ensure the greatest amount of people will understand and receive? In other words, am I preaching with the goal of effectiveness or am I am sticking to a style that just makes me comfortable?

- Using the framework Willow Creek developed in their Reveal study, I analyze the message that's forming in light of the four stages of spiritual maturity (Beginners, New Beginners, Close to Christ, Christ Centered). My purpose is to think of how each stage of maturity processes God's truth differently, so I want to be conscious of these differences.

- Is my sermon conversational? In other words, will people feel like I am talking with them or talking at them?

- Am I using language that is down to earth, and not "insider" language that only Christians understand?

In the end, the primary reason we should take the time to know our audience is not for the sake of developing a sermon, but so that we can pray for them. As you pray for your hearers, the burden of God for their souls will fill your heart with compassion. God's desire to cause a breakthrough in their lives will fill your heart. Bathing this step in prayer will help ensure that you won't just have a well-tailored sermon, but that your heart will love them before you begin to preach to them.

Take a few moments before we proceed to pray for your church, youth group, college outreach or whatever group of people God is calling you to preach to. Think of their faces, their stories and their life circumstances as you pray. Allow the Spirit of God to burden your soul for them. As you pray, I would encourage you to write down your prayers for them, taking note of how the Spirit is praying through you. I find these prayers play a huge role in the tone of my preaching. At times the things I find myself praying for may even show up in my actual sermon if it's appropriate.

With all this in mind, we are ready to begin to write our sermon. This is so exciting! God has been forming you to be his messenger throughout this entire process, but especially this last step. As you are now armed with the Gospel and a deep love for the people you will serve, you will soon have the joy of revealing the glory of God you have first experienced to thirsty and needy hearts. What a privilege it is to preach God's word!

Application:

1. Write down the names of four or five people in your church who are likely to be present when you preach. But most of all, write down the names of people who represent a cross-section of the kind of people who are part of your church. Intentionally select people that differ in age, ethnicity, career, life stage, socioeconomic background and spiritual maturity.

2. As you consider the message God has given you, take the time to think through how each of these differing people from step 1 will hear what you are saying. In other words, what will be the resistance to the Gospel from each of these people?

3. Take a prayer walk in your community. Take a notebook and write down what you see and experience.

4. Pay closer attention during pastoral conversations. What are you hearing beneath what's being verbally said? Allow that to lead you to pray.

STORY

Sometime during the fall of 2015 our family of churches (www.hopechurchnyc.org) had a joint service. It was a great day as together we celebrated all that God had done across our churches since the start of our family of churches in September 2012. What started out as 15 people at my friend Drew's rooftop had grown to a few hundred people across our city. I was in awe, and am still in awe, over all that God has done!

On that day, not only were our usual church members present, but we also had several visitors. Many of these visitors were friends of friends and came to celebrate alongside us and wish us well. Suffice it to say there were many people I didn't personally know that day. At the end of the service, I was introduced to a really tall, skinny gentleman. I don't normally focus on describing people in this kind of way, but when I say he was really tall and skinny, I need you to understand that he was really tall and really skinny!

Upon introductions he shook my hand. He was in mid conversation with someone else and was kind of interrupted by a friend who wanted him to meet me. As he turned in my direction and shook my hand he said, "Oh hey. Nice to meet you. I checked your website. I love your stories." He then turned away and returned to his conversation.

A few things registered quickly in my mind from that interaction. The first thing was that, though this was the first time I had met this guy, in a sense he had already met me by listening to one of my sermons. That was probably the first time I had ever met someone who had heard a sermon I preached but wasn't present at the church where I was preaching. It was a weird experience to be honest. Even though I preach a ton and have had the honor of preaching to many people, none of that has changed me from being a deep introvert. I would prefer being alone with a book on a bench somewhere or with a small handful of friends above being in the most extravagant of social settings. That moment felt weirdly vulnerable: this man had heard one of my sermons online and was able to form an opinion of me. He knew things about me without me ever having an equal opportunity to know him.

Another thing that registered in my mind is kind of embarrassing to admit. This admission will reveal how vain and puffed up I can be, so again it's embarrassing to confess this. Like that person who heard a sermon of mine and formed an opinion of me, as you read these words you will also be able to come to conclusions of me. I can't defend myself, clarify, give fuller context or nothing. This is an assault to my pride because I have actually never admitted this to anyone before. But here it goes.

My inner reaction to this man's words were "STORIES??? YOU LIKE MY STORIES? DON'T YOU MEAN MY SERMON? MY THEOLOGICALLY GROUNDED, CHRIST-CENTERED EXPOSITION OF SCRIPTURE? THE THING I PRAYED A TON OVER AND WORKED REALLY HARD ON? IS THAT WHAT YOU MEANT??" Behind my pleasant grin were these thoughts brewing. I was honestly offended a bit. My sense of calling, the gravitas of preaching were all ruffled at that moment. It's a good thing he turned away and didn't say anything more because I am from the streets and things could have gotten sticky! Just kidding, or am I?

In full disclosure, I am a sensitive guy, but I'm generally not that sensitive. To my ear his comment felt a bit condescending and as a result it triggered something in me. You see, I deeply value the act of preaching. I hold it in high regard, so the feeling that it was being referred to in a negative light was troublesome to me. That being said, since that was long ago and I have had some time to reflect on my internal reaction, I've come to realize that what bothered me had less to do with his tone or even my sensitivity, and it had more to do with my view of a sermon.

To me, a sermon is the exposition of Scripture. Sure it has anecdotes, stories, and humor, but it is deeply theological. Our experience as people is definitely a grid through which God's word will travel on its way to one's heart, so a sermon has some autobiographical elements. I get all that, but to call it a "story" felt too lowbrow for me. It didn't feel lofty enough. It lacked the proper aura that a Christ-centered sermon should have.

A lot has changed for me since that day. I'm happy to report that after serving as a lead pastor since December 2015 my ego is not as sensitive as it was then. God has humbled me, broken me, and repaired me many times over during this season. What has also changed is my perspective on how I view a sermon. If I stumbled into that gentleman again today and we had the same interaction and he said, "I like your stories," this time around I would grab him by the shirt and pin him to the ground and scream at him.

Just kidding. This time around I would have a grin as big as my face can form and I would say, "Thank you! That's awfully kind of you to say."

I've come to realize that an effective sermon is in essence a well told story. Clearly this story is anchored in a text of Scripture, it focuses on Christ, it points to the greater narrative of Scripture and declares the Gospel, and it confronts idols, but it does all this in the form of a story. You see, if God is telling his story throughout the Bible, and if the work of Christ is called the Gospel (Good News), to preach in a non-narrative format is a different communication medium than the way the original message is told in Scripture. This is not to say that sermons should be void of didactic teaching or lack the elements of a lecture. There is a place and a need for that, but I would argue that didactic teaching and lecture should be elements within the story we are telling rather than being the actual form of our sermon.

There is a vast difference between a sermon that has stories in it versus a sermon that feels like a story from start to finish. People process and internalize stories in a very deep manner. We absorb them in ways that other forms of communication just can't compare. When our sermons are not shaped like stories, there are certain things we will say that won't stand a chance of being internalized by our hearers.

Now if you're like me, all this story talk can make you feel nervous because it could give the impression that we have to be master storytellers in order to preach effective sermons. If this were the standard we need to meet, that would place an insane amount of pressure on us, especially if we are not natural storytellers. In addition, this focus on being a great storyteller can feel pretty close to simply being an entertainer. If you are feeling any of those tensions, I have good news. The call to preach narrative sermons is not a call that only a few, highly gifted orators can answer.

What gives each of us an advantage to preaching story-esque sermons is that our God is a storyteller. From the very first words of the Bible where it says "In the beginning God," we are introduced to a God who is telling a story and inviting us into it. When Christ enters our world as a vulnerable baby, grows up and begins to preach, his style of communicating was to tell stories in the form of parables. The substance of our faith is given to us through the medium of stories, so when it comes to preaching sermons that are more like stories, the medium of stories fits all too well with the message we are proclaiming.

Our desire to increase engagement through effective storytelling is not for the sake of fame or admiration, but solely for the sake of people being transformed. If we help increase the engagement people have with Scripture through storytelling, it can be argued that we are helping to increase the degree of transformation people can experience.

Though some preachers are naturally more engaging than others, in the end there is no excuse for not being engaging in some way, shape or form. When Paul says in 1 Corinthians 9 that he became all things to all people in order to win some to Christ, he was describing a disposition that all Christians should have, but especially preachers. If learning how to grow as an engaging communicator could help more people encounter God, then regardless of how tough that work may be, it's our responsibility to say yes to this opportunity.

Eugene Lowry in his book *The Homiletical Plot: The Sermon as Narrative Art Form* offers incredible insights on how to preach engaging, story-form messages. Lowry talks about "disturbing the equilibrium" as being one of the first things preachers should do. One of the ways he explains this concept is by pointing out that as preachers we should assume that no one who is present in our churches is actually ready or desirous to follow us on the journey that is our sermon. As a pastor, I have to say this idea is counterintuitive because my assumption is that by virtue of their presence on a Sunday they want to go where the sermon will take them. Isn't that why they are there? What Lowry helps us understand is that people come to church carrying all sorts of baggage. Their week was likely a bit crazy, their commute to the Sunday gathering might have been challenging and with so many other things they are juggling, it's pastorally wise to assume they need to be lovingly invited to come along for the voyage.

Disturbing the equilibrium involves creating engagement from the very outset of the sermon by introducing narrative tension. Lowry contrasts a movie with the average sermon in order to highlight the proper use of narrative tension. He aptly points out that if the opening scenes of a movie were similar to most sermons, the result would be that the theater would empty out after only a few moments. Many sermons begin by telling people what they are going to be about, may even highlight key points and may even allude to the application. To be fair, I get why pastors do this. Nothing is more frustrating for a pastor than to hear someone walk away with confusion regarding the core idea of your sermon. We want people to have a clear understanding of what we will be talking about, so the simplest way to accomplish this is to plainly tell them from the outset. Lowry argues that by starting our sermons in this manner it would be equivalent to the opening scenes of a movie revealing the plot and giving indications on how the narrative tension would be resolved. That would never happen in a movie because directors understand that without managing and leveraging tension, moviegoers would lack reasonable motivation to sit through the entire movie. Why should they? If they know how the story will be resolved from the outset, why would they waste their time and wait for the movie to unfold?

Similar to how a story is structured and told, Lowry argues that our sermons should employ the same form, beginning with our introduction. Our sermon intro should disturb the equilibrium by introducing tension. The beginning of our sermon should create curiosity, causing people to ask, "Where are we going?" They are asking this question not because we are confusing them and they feel lost, but because our introduction of narrative tension lets them know we are heading somewhere that has yet to be revealed. Whether through a question, a story, a joke, etc. we begin our sermon by awakening people's imaginations by sharing something that stirs their hearts to want to know more.

The second step in Lowry's process is to dig deeper into the tension. He calls this "analyzing the tension." In essence we want to hover around the tension we have introduced so we can look at it from multiple angles. This act of hovering over the tension and analyzing it heightens engagement in addition to paving the way for eventual understanding. The last thing we want to do in a sermon is provide answers to questions people are not asking. As interesting as we may find the subject we are dealing with, without introducing tension that leads to engagement, people's minds will not be hungry for answers. Giving answers to questions not being asked is one of the best examples of a boring sermon.

As in every good story, once the equilibrium has been disturbed and the tension has been thoroughly analyzed, the next step is to introduce the solution. It may take some time for the solution to fully play out in the story, but at a certain point it's definitely introduced. Lowry calls this third step "disclosing the clue to resolution" or "exploring the solution." At this point in our sermon, we introduce the solution from God's word and begin the process of exploring what it means. The tension has been building in people's hearts. At this point they are yearning for relief.

This stage in a sermon is akin to the slow rise of a roller coaster before that first initial drop. Anticipation has been building as they slowly approach the edge of no return. In a sermon people know God is taking them somewhere through his word, but they are not quite sure exactly where they are going. They have been staring at the tension from multiple angles and have analyzed it thoroughly. During this process their souls have come to a place where they are craving resolution. If they weren't on board with you when you first started, by now they are bought in and really want to know how things will be resolved. In the roller coaster analogy, they have climbed to the very top of the ascent and for the first time in this journey they have a glimpse of where this ride is heading. Milliseconds later the coaster drops and everyone starts screaming in a mixture of joy and horror. The build up is finally over and now the momentum of those first moments will carry them forward to the end of the ride.

Hopefully Lowry's process has been helpful to you thus far. But if it's not connecting for you I would also suggest Andy Stanley's process in *Communicating for a Change*. Similar to Lowry's flow or structure, Stanley also has five movements in his structure. Though he uses very different language than Lowry, I actually think they are very similar in their essence, though I do think that Stanley's template is far more memorable and quite effective.

Andy Stanley's proposed sermon structure is Me, We, God, You, We. In the Me section of the sermon, we are introducing ourselves and the issue we are going to deal with. This takes place during the intro of your sermon. Next is the We section of your sermon. In this next step we are seeking to bring to light how both ourselves as the preacher and them as the audience each share a common struggle with the issue that was raised in the Me section. Our goal in these first two steps is to raise tension and stir a desire for that tension to be resolved, so that once we've done that we are now ready for the third step, which is the God section of the sermon. This is the portion of the sermon where we offer the biblical truth that helps resolve the tension we have been raising and provides answers to our struggle. The next step is the You section of the sermon that deals with application. We are basically asking the question "Now that you know what God's word says, what are You going to do with it?" Once you outline what application looks like, the last section is the We section of the sermon where we paint a picture of what our lives corporately as the people of God would look like if we obey God in this area.

Though there are two more steps in Lowry's process, for the purposes of this chapter we are going to stop here. We will touch on the remaining steps of Lowry's process in the next chapter.

Another helpful resource in shaping sermons into stories is Chip and Dan Heath's book *Made to Stick*. I highly recommend this book for people who want to grow in their ability to communicate. The authors of this book argue that there are six elements to communication that is "sticky", i.e. communication that connects and is memorable. The first element is simplicity. The question that drives us toward simplicity is "How do you strip an idea to its core without turning it into a silly sound bite?" The next element is unexpectedness. Sticky communication leverages unexpectedness to create tension and increase engagement. The question we are asking in this step is "How do you capture people's attention and hold it?"

Next is the idea of concreteness. The question we are asking here is "How do you help people understand your idea and remember it much later?" Establishing credibility is the next element and is a vital key to sticky communication. In this step we are asking "How do you get people to believe your idea?" Next is how to communicate in a way that is emotional. This step is concerned with the question "How do you get people to care about your idea?" Unless people care, our ideas won't move them. Communicating with emotion in a way that connects with their emotions is key to getting folks to care. Lastly is the use of stories. In this step we are asking "How do you get people to act on your idea?"

When crafting sermons, the categories the Heath brothers raise are incredibly helpful to consider, as are the insights of many other books on the subject of effective communication. I would encourage every preacher to study the art of effective storytelling from every credible resource out there. There are many *Ted* talks that offer helpful tips on this subject. Learn as much as you can from anyone that offers useful info.

I have found the practice of following up every abstract, theoretical statement with an analogy, story, anecdote, etc. to be very helpful in making my sermon much more a narrative. A friend of mine once shared with me the insight that he gleaned from either Spurgeon or some other preacher (my memory fails me on this) that for every seven minutes of preaching there should be some type of story. I raise this idea not to chain you to that specific format, but more so to highlight the discipline of inserting narrative devices throughout your sermon so that it remains rooted in a narrative flow.

Though I have suggested several books and *Ted* talks, I realize the idea of reading more on this particular aspect of narrative preaching may seem a bit taxing. Just in case reading more books and watching videos seems daunting, I want to offer some suggestions on creating an outline that I have found helpful.

1. Create engaging introductions. In the first few moments of your sermon I would work on engaging people, hooking them in. Whether it's a story, a question you pose, a joke you share, a statistic you highlight. There are many ways you can create an engaging intro. These are just a few. Get creative and have fun.

2. Connect deeply to the text. Once the introduction is complete, it's time to dive into the text, but doing this should be done to deepen the tension we have introduced in our intro. As we share the historical context of the passage, the author's intent, details about the original audience, the grammatical nuances found in the original language and all the other elements of exegesis, we should seek to do so with the goal of fostering greater engagement. We are sharing information, but we are building a case for why they should focus in and hear more.

3. Crystalize the main idea. Once we have created that tension and shared the findings from our exegesis, we should share plainly what we are seeking to address through our sermon. We aren't yet answering the question we are raising, but at this point we are plainly stating the question we will answer.

4. Reveal Christ and Declare the Gospel. The transformative power in our messages will always be how Christ is revealed and how the Gospel is proclaimed. In seeking to answer the questions that have been raised from the text we are preaching from, our joy is to proclaim how Christ uniquely addresses those questions and how the Gospel empowers us to walk out the revelation of Christ.

5. Expose Idols and Point to Obedience. Once we have proclaimed Christ and his Gospel, it behooves us to highlight our resistance to Christ and the Good News. Whatever those idols may be, they need to be exposed and brought to light in order for us to repent from them. Christ and the Gospel are beautiful enough that if idols are exposed people will see the inferiority in comparison to Christ. As they let go of their idols, their hearts are ready for instruction on obedience. Be clear with application. We should point people towards obedience that is a response to the Gospel, obedience that is a response to what Christ has done.

Though these are five steps, I like to think of these five steps as taking place over three movements that are closely related to the narrative arc of most stories and movies. Steps 1-3 are part of the first movement that seeks to introduce narrative tension. Steps 4 is the climax of the story as we focus on who Christ is and the power of his Gospel. Step 5 is the resolution of the story as we dissect the idols that keep us from experiencing the completion Christ and the Gospel provide. In the last movement we want to paint a picture of how Christ restores us to the point of walking in obedience.

In terms of what your actual outline looks like, there is so much freedom in this. Some folks love to manuscript their sermon, detailing every word they will say, which helps them to preach narratively. Others prefer bullet point outlines that only provide the skeletal frame for what they will flesh out. In the end, I would explore both of these options and any others you might find helpful. Whatever form of outline that helps you to preach the story of God faithfully, that's what should determine your actual outline.

Once you land on an outline, I would encourage you to preach it aloud a couple of times. This step is helpful because often what looks good as the written word doesn't translate well as the preached word. The best way to find that out is to preach your outline aloud and see how it sounds and feels. During this exercise you are wanting to find out what isn't clear in your delivery. Remember, people won't have the luxury of reading your words as you preach, so anything that is confusing will remain confusing. Because of this we want to be as clear as possible in what we say and how we say it. After you practice at least once, that will help you determine what should remain in your outline, what should be removed and what needs some tweaking.

The more often you preach, the step of preaching your sermon aloud to yourself becomes less necessary as a formal act because your mind tends to get an intuitive sense of what parts of your outline won't work for actual preaching. However, for people just starting to preach, or if you are preaching on a rotation of once every few weeks, I would suggest making this step part of your regimen. The repetition will help you work out kinks even before you step into a pulpit, but it will also increase your confidence as a preacher as the sermon becomes internalized in your soul.

With all this good work under your belt, you are now prepared to preach, but there still remains one important last step. Though this last step is one word, it has two sides to it. One of the sides of this last step we have lightly touched on. When we spell it out it will be clear that we have already alluded to it, but the other side of this next step is sadly not spoken of often,

Without further ado, let's dive into the last step in this preaching matrix.

Application:

1. How are you going to intro your sermon?

2. What are the key ideas/concepts that your exegesis has unearthed for you?

3. What is the central point of your sermon? Write it down in a clear and succinct sentence. Don't stop working on your sermon till you achieve that kind of clarity.

4. How will Christ be revealed through your sermon?

5. What are the idols that will be confronted in the hearts of listeners?

6. What point of obedience are people being called to through your sermon?

EXPECTATION

Managing expectations seems to be the go-to strategy for people who have experienced deep disappointments. I have lost count the amount of times I have heard people say, "If you have high expectations of others, you will always be let down. The key to life is to have low expectations, ideally no expectations and you will never be disappointed." Most of the people I have heard say these words have had somewhat of a grin on their face as they relish in the brilliance of what sounds like great wisdom. The look on their face is a sort of basking in what feels akin to people having discovered the fountain of youth or a secret elixir that solves all of life's woes. Without using so many words, their face seems to imply that they feel sorry for all those bozos who still have expectations of others and as a result remain susceptible to being hurt.

I get where they are coming from, and though I disagree with their conclusions, I don't judge because this protectionist philosophy makes sense on some levels. If you have no expectations of others, you won't be disappointed. Your hopes in others will never be dashed if you don't have hopes to begin with. Though this strategy can shield you from many of life's disappointments, it comes with a high cost, namely the numbing of our souls.

We are not living a fully human life if we choose to live a life with no expectations, placing no hope in others. Not only does this posture dehumanize us personally, but it also dehumanizes others. It's been said that people naturally rise to our highest expectation of them. I have found this to be true regarding the expectations people have placed on me. Something comes alive in us when people see the potential inside us and call it out. Rising to the expectations of others (if those expectations are reasonable, shared in love and coupled with support and encouragement) can cause amazing growth in our lives. We become better, stronger, and a deeper version of our true selves when expectations are placed upon us with grace.

Sadly, the converse is devastatingly true. When we have low expectations or no expectations of ourselves, we settle for less than we should and allow potential to lay undeveloped. The same is true for the expectations we have of others and the expectations others have of us. Something dies in people when we can't see who they are beyond their struggles and beyond their present reality. The loss we experience when this happens is not just personal, rather it spills over into our relationships, the businesses we lead and the organizations we serve. Everyone loses when the power of expectation is not leveraged for the flourishing of others.

When it comes to preaching God's word, I believe more sermons have been negatively impacted by a lack of expectation than can be accurately assessed. I would argue that even when a sermon is theologically sound, it still has the potential to fall flat due to low expectations. As we close out this DECREASE preaching matrix, this issue of expectation is a hinge of sorts on which all of our prayer and studying for our sermon swing.

The absence of expectation in sermons is twofold. It's helpful to think of expectation from the perspective of our listeners and from the perspective of us as preachers. Let's first unpack the idea of expectation from the perspective of our listeners.

"What does God expect people to do?" That was the question Rick Paladin, Pastor of Word & Worship Church in Pittsburgh, PA shared with me several years ago. I had called Rick to pick his brain on how their multi-site church cooked up sermons across several locations, where each congregation of people listening to a live preacher. I was familiar with the concept of video venue, where one preacher is simulcasted to many locations, multiplying the impact and reach of that one preacher. But what Rick was doing was new for me. I was curious how it worked. During our conversation he shared that his sermons weren't ready to be preached until he could clearly answer two questions. The first question is "What is God saying?" and the other is "What does God expect people to do?"

At this point in sermon preparation, we should be able to to clearly answer the first question. We have spent considerable time and energy beholding God as well as thinking through what he is calling us to preach. As we have considered the people God has called us to share the Good News with and honed in on our storied sermon structure, we should be able to confidently answer the first question.

Though the question of what God is saying is of the utmost importance, if we don't answer the second question we are not yet ready to preach. Answering the question "What does God expect people to do" is a crucial step to take before we enter the pulpit. That answer should powerfully shape the intent of the sermon and our posture as a preacher. Failing to answer that question before we preach can be detrimental because it can reduce the sermon from a proclamation of God's heart to nothing more than a religious lecture. If your sermon is reduced to a lecture, regardless of how filled with sound theological content it might be, it will lack the power to call people to a response of obedience.

People can pick and choose what they like or don't like from a lecture, and in our culture that's exactly what they will do. But as we enter the pulpit, we come armed with more than nice suggestions and religious facts. Rather we come with fire in our souls from the living God. Our privilege is to call people to worship Christ in light of who he is and what he has done. Our aim has never been to entertain or tickle their ears.

The first aspect of expectation is having clarity on the matter of application. Based on what God is saying through his word, how are his people supposed to apply what they are hearing in their lives? The goal of a sermon should to be exalt Christ before our hearers to the point that his beauty and glory melts the stubbornness of their hearts, paving the way for heartfelt, Spirit-empowered obedience.

The book of James has some profound words in this regard. James 1:22-25 says:

"Do not merely listen to the word, and so deceive yourselves. Do what it says. Anyone who listens to the word but does not do what it says is like someone who looks at his face in a mirror and, after looking at himself, goes away and immediately forgets what he looks like. But whoever looks intently into the perfect law that gives freedom, and continues in it—not forgetting what they have heard, but doing it—they will be blessed in what they do."

There is a danger in simply listening to God's word and not obeying it. James says the practice of listening to God's word and not obeying is rooted in self-deception. That's a pretty shocking statement. A person could be listening to God's holy, life-altering, grace-filled word and at that very moment find themselves captive to self deception. Kind of terrifying if you ask me!

How is it possible to be in earshot of God's liberating word, yet the result of hearing that word is bondage, marked by deception?

For starters, hearing God's word can be such a holy moment that, unless we consciously decide to obey what we are hearing, we can be left thinking "that was powerful...that was so true...glad I heard that!" and easily end up doing nothing. I remember attending a workshop hosted by Stephen Covey focusing on the principles of his book *The 7 Habits of Highly Effective People*. It was brilliant content! With each section, I felt like my life was coming into clearer focus. Goals and dreams that once felt so far away now seemed like I could reach out and touch them with my fingertips. My heart was racing, my eyes were focused, my adrenaline was pumping as the mountains of obstacles were becoming like small dust piles. All of this was happening as the *Rocky* soundtrack was playing in my head (I have quite the imagination). I was so pumped during that workshop it took everything in me not to scream out "EYE OF THE TIGER IT'S THE THRILL OF THE FIGHT!!"

But there was one problem, a rather big problem. For all my excitement about conquering the world and after metaphorically pouring Gatorade over my head, I had done absolutely nothing to achieve any of my goals. Sure I was excited, but that didn't mean anything had actually changed. Was I feeling pumped? You bet! Did that enthusiasm have any tangible fruit? Sadly, no. It was all just concepts. No doubt they were powerful concepts, principles that could change my life if I applied them. Yet until I actually incorporated them into my life, they would remain ethereal, nothing more.

Many people have a similar experience in our churches. The preached word excites them, stirs them and paints a picture of what life could be like if God was at the center of their lives. But nothing changes until they obey what they are hearing. Sadly, we have churches filled with Christians who hear sermons like no one's business. If hearing sermons and not obeying what God is teaching us was an Olympic sport, our folks would outshine Michael Phelps! With the proliferation of podcasts and sermons via social media, these days many Christians consume way more sermons than ever before in history. Though that's good and necessary, the question will always remain: what does God expect you to do?

Dave Ferguson once wrote that most Christians have 3-5 years of doctrinal information beyond their present level of obedience. Ouch! Can I get an amen on that one? No? Too soon? Okay, I digress. Let's get back to that quote. Think about that idea. Most Christians have more doctrinal information than they are presently obeying. This quote paints a troubling picture of followers of Jesus who possibly know how to quote Jesus till the cows come home, yet never bother to obey him.

I think the other aspect of deception implied in James 1 is thinking we actually have the freedom to choose if and what we will obey from God's word. It's an audacious posture to have before God that says "Thanks for that insight, God. I will think that over and will get back to you if I choose to follow through with that." I wish this was hyperbole and only describing the broader, non-Christian culture that surrounds us, but sadly this description is applicable to many Christians - Christians who faithfully attend our churches and even take notes while we preach. We have a generation of Christians who think it's their right to choose if they will be racists or not, choose if God's sexual ethics are something they will entertain, consider if generosity is a practice they could see themselves possibly practicing, and are going to explore if forgiving others is a command that fits into their priorities. It's bad out here!

When we cherry pick what we deem worthy of obeying, we reveal the heart of all sin, namely the exalting of ourselves to the place of God. Only God has the authority and power to declare right from wrong, righteousness from unrighteousness. When we take on that role of being the arbiter of truth, it's the highest form of pride.

Jesus was no salesman. Though filled with grace, mercy and compassion, Jesus was not trying to build a following at any cost. In fact, John 5 tells us that his message of sacrificial obedience and commitment was so intense that a crowd of thousands shrunk to 12. Only 12! If that wasn't eventful enough for one day, Jesus proceeded to confront the remaining 12 (his hand-chosen apostles) and challenged them directly with a call to a high commitment of obedience. Like the preaching of Jesus, our preaching should not shy away from a call to obedience, even if it means we lose favor with people.

In Matthew 16:24 we read, "Then Jesus said to his disciples, 'Whoever wants to be my disciple must deny themselves and take up their cross and follow me.'" There is no sugarcoating in this declaration. The blow is not softened, we are offered no anesthesia. Following Jesus is an invitation to carry a cross as we pursue the Master. Christ tells us that following him will require denying ourselves as we bear our cross. Imagine that? There was no promise of our potential being fulfilled, our lives being maximized for greatness, and getting everything we ever wanted. Discipleship is not an invitation with the promise that God will co-sign all of our desires and life's decisions. Following Jesus is a journey fueled by the words "not my will, but your will be done" with each unfolding step.

If our sermons only highlight the cross of Jesus, then there is one cross too few. Before you stone me for being a heretic, please allow me to clarify. Only the cross of Jesus contains the power to save sinners through the power of God's grace and love. That cross should always, and must always be held high for all to see. But if that is the only cross we hold up during our preaching, then our Gospel will not be complete because we will be proclaiming a savior who died for our sins without ever calling sinners to repent of their sins. The second cross we must hold up in our sermons is the cross of repentance and faith towards God, and our communication of what God expects us to do is a direct invitation towards that.

Before we tackle the second aspect of expectation, here are some final thoughts on this first aspect. As you prepare to deliver your sermon, what is the application that flows from God's word that you will be calling people to? If your message is on forgiveness, what does the application look like? If your message is on faith, what does obedience to God in that area look like? Until you are clear on what the application will be, you are not yet ready to preach. But after all this time spent in prayer and study, I'm confident that the application is practically leaping off the page.

Take a moment and write down what God is expecting people to do. As you write it down, take some time to pray about how you are supposed to call people towards that particular obedience. Though it will be said with love and grace, if you are like me this can be a moment filled with trepidation. No one ultimately likes to be told to obey someone else, even if that someone else happens to be God. It can be intimidating to call people to carry their cross in obedience, but take heart! It's not you that is ultimately calling them to carry their cross, for you and I are only simply messengers. Our job is to deliver the news, not choose which news we will deliver.

The good news is that, though the cross of obedience can be a tough one to pick up, the disciple's cross is nothing more than a response to the Savior's cross. In other words, though it's a big deal to pick up our cross and follow Jesus, it pales in comparison to the cross he bore for us. Framing our obedience as a response to His redemptive sacrifice removes the pressure from calling people to repentance and faith because, in light of his cross, the disciples' cross is the only reasonable and fitting response.

Having established the first aspect of expectation, let's move on to the second aspect. This second aspect of expectation concerns the heart of the preacher as they prepare to enter into the pulpit. As I explain, you won't be reading anything new, but you will be reading about something that is sorely missing from many sermons.

Divine expectation. That's the best way I can describe the second aspect of expectation. What I mean by this is best understood in the form of a question: "What is your divine expectation as you approach the pulpit?" A simple question with profound implications. But just in case it's not apparent what I mean by "divine expectation," let's unpack it together.

As you have spent time with God during each step of this process, I'm confident that something more than sermon ideas have entered your heart. Perhaps a catchy phrase has been penned, a pregnant statement is ready to be uttered, and a clear theological conviction has been formed during this process. All of these are good things, things we thank God for, but thankfully that's not the ultimate movement that has been taking place in your soul. God has been shaping a message in your heart during this whole process, and with each line and layer of this message, he has been depositing something powerful in you, and your faith has been rising in a commensurate manner. Alongside the message God has been revealing to you, he has also been creating a sense of expectancy in your soul. Divine expectancy!

Divine expectation in preaching is the faith God has placed in your heart for what his word will soon accomplish. More than just relaying information, the act of preaching releases God's thoughts, and with God's thoughts come God's power to create God's purposes in the lives of people. God has chosen to use the preaching of his word to accomplish his work,. As we prepare to preach, God will arm us with an expectation for what he desires to accomplish.

When I think of preaching, Genesis 1 speaks to me strongly. In the opening scenes of Scripture we are given our first glance at the nature and being of God. Upon gazing at God in this text, we are struck as we discover that God is a creator. Our God first reveals himself as creator. Think about how profound this is. God is a creator! Everything we see in this world was the work of our Father, the architect and general contractor of the universe. He not only designed it all, he created it all.

One of the things that strikes me about this opening scene in Genesis is the means by which God creates the universe, namely by speaking. Through the speaking of words, God's power is unleashed. Things that once did not exist in the material world come to being. This act of creation is distinct from all other acts of creation in that God was creating everything we see from things that had yet to exist. The Latin phrase for this moment of creation is *ex nihilo* which means "out of nothing." When you and I create, we have the luxury of taking things that exist and morphing them into different things. All of our creative acts are taking place on the canvas of God's original creation. We are not originators in our works of creation; at best we are glorious imitators of the first creator, God himself.

This passages speaks deeply to me about the act of preaching because I believe preaching is fundamentally a creative act. When I refer to preaching as a "creative act," it would be easy to assume that I'm referring to the creativity it takes to preach an engaging message that utilizes effective analogies and memorable stories. But I'm not referring to any of that.

Preaching as a creative act has nothing to do with us, and everything to do with God. Through preaching God is creating his purposes in the hearts of people. Graces, desires, motivations, freedom, conviction, faith and joy that once did not exist in people are being created through the preaching of God's word.

God calls us to deliver more than just information about him; he invites us to be co-creators of his plans in this world through the act of preaching. What an invitation! What a holy work that is embedded in sermons.

Divine expectation for what God will do through preaching certainly develops during our times of preparation. But in actuality it begins long before we even begin to prepare to preach. Luke 4:18-19 tells us of the moment Jesus enters the synagogue and grabs the scroll of the Prophet Isaiah and reads Isaiah 61:1-2. This passage foretells that one day a Messiah would come and declare good news to the poor, sight for the blind, liberty to the captive and freedom for the oppressed. What a promise! Israel waited a long time for the day when the world would be restored, and they would be redeemed. Upon grabbing the scroll, he reads the words of Isaiah and says, "Today this scripture is fulfilled in your hearing" and sits down. What an electrifying moment! Christ is declaring that he is the promised Messiah. And as only God would do, he sits down like a boss!

Many refer to Luke 4:18-19 as the mission statement of Jesus. This passage spells out why he has come and to whom he has come. The hope for the restoration of the world is found in this passage. Through the message Christ would preach, the acts of love he would share, the miracles he would perform and ultimately his death, burial, resurrection, ascension and the sending of his Spirit, Good News would be available for all.

While it's right to focus on the "why" of Jesus' mission found in this text, often we overlook the "how" of his ministry, namely the anointing of the Spirit. Though born supernaturally as Mary was found with child through the Spirit of God, it's interesting that the ministry of Jesus did not begin at his supernatural birth, but rather it began at the waters of his baptism when the Spirit came upon him. This is noteworthy for us: what made the ministry of Jesus possible was not his virgin birth, something none of us can share with him. Rather the power behind the ministry of Jesus was made possible through the anointing of the Spirit of God. Praise God for that because all of us partake of that same anointing!

The starting place of divine expectation is not all the prayer and fasting you have engaged in for your sermon; the starting place is in the act of God of making you his child and sealing you with his Spirit. That's good news if you have ever preached a sermon where you weren't able to pray as you would have hoped for, but it's humbling news if you feel like you prayed more than the angels. Divine expectation doesn't rest on efforts, rather it abides in us, namely through the indwelling of the Spirit of God.

The moment the Holy Spirit came to indwell your heart by faith you were anointed by the same Spirit that anointed Jesus Christ himself. In fact, Romans 8:11 says that "if the Spirit of him that raised Jesus from the dead lives in your mortal body, he shall by that same Spirit give life to your mortal bodies." Did you catch that? The Spirit that raised Jesus from the dead lives in you, imparting divine life into your mortal body.

In Acts 1:8 Jesus tells his disciples that, when the Spirit is poured out upon them, they shall receive power to be his witnesses. That word "power" is the word *dunamis* from which we get the word dynamite. Jesus is telling his disciples that the Spirit will impart an explosive power and authority to proclaim who he is. This promise of power was not just for the apostles, rather it is for every follower of Jesus, but particularly present when we are proclaiming the Gospel.

The first element of divine expectation is the resident anointing upon you by virtue of being his child. You don't earn that or work for that. The second element of divine expectation is the stirring of faith that has come as a result of the message God has been placing in your heart. You are first and foremost anointed as his child, but God also places an anointing for the message you will preach. Both the messenger and the message are anointed by the Spirit. In order for God to create his purposes in our broken world through flawed messengers, we need every bit of anointing God will give.

What are you expecting God to do through your sermon? What will God create? With each prayer you have prayed, each passage you have dissected, each revealing of Christ you have received, each connection to God's bigger story, each illumination of the Gospel you have seen, expectation has been rising. It's not presumptuous to drive your stake in the ground and say "I believe God will do X" based on your status as his child, but also on your calling as his messenger.

In many ways we seek to be humble and open to the mysterious work of God in the way we frame our faith around his purposes. Despite the many ways people try to control God, even as Christians we are powerless in that regard. God will do whatever he desires, even if we want him to do something entirely different. We can't bend his arm and coerce him to do anything, even when we are asking him to do good things. God determines his own will and conforms all things after his will. It's all on him, so it makes total sense for us to have a posture of humble, open faith.

Though there are so many things we will never see or understand regarding how God works through sermons, as we approach the pulpit we need both humble and open faith. But we also need tenacious, bold and specific faith.

As much as we should seek to avoid presumption on what God will do, in the case of preaching it's not presumption to believe that God will do a specific work based on the message he is giving you to preach from his word.

My pastor, Bishop Joseph Mattera, would drill this truth in my soul from the moment I began to preach. He would tell me that, whatever he was preaching on, he would believe God was going to do a work in conjunction with that message. If he was preaching on prayer, he believed that people would receive a desire to pray from the Spirit of God. If the sermon was on forgiveness, he believed God wanted to set people free from the burden of unforgiveness. As a young man I had a front row seat to his ministry as I watched God do some amazing things. I learned during those days that God's word is alive.

Hebrews 4:12 says "For the word of God is alive and active. Sharper than any double-edged sword, it penetrates even to dividing soul and spirit, joints and marrow; it judges the thoughts and attitudes of the heart." God's word is ALIVE and ACTIVE. It's SHARPER than any double-edged sword. Did you catch that? Sharper than ANY double-edged sword. God's word PENETRATES and DIVIDES soul and spirit and it JUDGES the thoughts and attitudes of the heart.

When God describes his word in this manner, how could it be even remotely possible for us to preach with little-to-no expectation for what God will do? To preach with no expectation in our hearts is to lack a clear understanding of who God is and the nature of his word.

I wish it wasn't the case, but it seems many sermons are preached with no expectation. At the heart-level of the preacher, the sermon is delivered not much differently than other forms of communication. It could be engaging, biblical and even have an articulation of Gospel in it, yet there is a disconnect because there is no sense of expectation in the preacher.

You may be wondering how I could feel comfortable making such a broad judgment? Perhaps you may be asking how could I make such a subjective claim as fact?

I speak to many pastors, many who preach often. Some of these conversations are immediately before they preach. I can tell you firsthand that as pastors we are not always entering the pulpit with fire in our bones. We all long for it, but it isn't always there for a host a reasons, none of which are on God's part. Many pastors have to deal with so many pressing issues that having singular focus on preaching is quite challenging. We are often hurried due to the many tasks we are juggling and our hearts are at times bruised by the very people to whom we seek to feed God's word. Our loved ones struggle with all sorts of challenges, and our own souls are bombarded by a myriad of Satan's attacks. If you are a pastor, this is not news to you. But if you aren't a pastor, I hope this prompts you to pray for your pastor often. If you aspire to be a pastor, I hope this provides some sobriety as you prepare for the trials within a life of ministry.

Divine expectation is lacking in preaching in large part because most sermons are not developed prayerfully nor are they delivered prayerfully. In our most honest moments, pastors will admit we struggle to maintain a vibrant prayer life. Not only does this show up in other areas of our lives, but it definitely shows up in our preaching. When all we are doing is sharing some thoughts we have on a text, why would we ever really need to pray to do that? If you have been preaching for some time now, I would argue that it's probably easier for you to preach mechanically, relying on your past memories of how God met you and his people during other prayerful sermons. Without much prayerful preparation we will more than likely be performing a sermon, rather than proclaiming it.

Not only does our lack of prayer impact our expectation, but the way we study God's word can also limit our experience of divine expectation. If the way we study Scripture is not rooted in a strong discipline of exegesis and Christ-centeredness, it's hard to imagine how our sermons would ever be marked with a Spirit-empowered expectation. We receive expectation from God as we encounter him in his word. But if we are not digging into his word until it begins to dig into us, it will likely remain in the realm of a lecture rather than an anointed sermon. As God's word dives deeply into our hearts through our times of prayer and study, God begins to deposit the seeds of expectation through the truths he is illuminating to our hearts. Unless we are approaching God's word with this posture, it will be next to impossible for a biblical, divine expectation to take root in us.

As I began to write this book, I can't tell you how many struggles I have faced along the way. Many of these challenges tempted me to give up and just delete every word I had typed. I gave up and restarted many times over on this book. Despite these obstacles, there was one thing that kept me pushing forward: a very distinct hope, specifically around this idea of divine expectation.

My hope is that God would use this book in some small way to renew, as well as spark for the very first time, a sense of divine expectation for what God can do through the work of preaching. The prayer of my heart has been that in my lifetime I would see us preachers walk in a deeper faith in the power of God at work through our preaching. Imagine if every sermon that is preached is drenched in a sense of expectation in light of the power of Christ and the power of his Gospel. Just imagine the things God would do through preachers who preached with that kind of faith!

We've come to the end of our journey in the DECREASE preaching matrix. At this point you are now ready to stand behind a pulpit and declare to others the glory of Christ that you have been beholding first as his child. Those intimate moments with the Father have forged a Gospel proclamation in your soul, first to you, but now it will be shared through you. Through much prayer, love and thought you have listened to God as you have considered the people he has called you to serve as well as the very structure of the message you will proclaim. The ribbon on top of all this wonderful work is a clear expectation as to what people will be called to do in light of what God has been revealing through his word. Armed with clear application for this message, your soul is also stirred with a sense of faith as to what God is about to do. His purposes and plans will be created in the hearts of people through the sermon you will preach. What a mysterious, humbling, purely amazing thing that is about to take place!

You are ready to preach. But, more aptly, God has prepared you to preach as he has been the one molding you all along for this sacred task. As you enter the pulpit, I pray you do so with deep humility and utter confidence the same God that raised Christ from the dead has anointed you for this moment. The love God has imparted in your soul for his people is but a fraction of what God directly feels for his people, so take comfort, for their sake, that God is way more invested in the fruitfulness of your sermon than you could ever be. God will be glorified through your sermon, and the best part of all is that, whether you are praised or denigrated for the message you're about to share, it really makes no difference to your soul. Why is that the case? Because you have beheld the glory of God and nothing will ever compare, nothing will even come close to who Jesus is. As long as he is on the throne, everything else is but dust in light of eternity.

Have fun. Don't take yourself too seriously. Take God utterly seriously. Sit back and watch God do amazing things. Go forth and preach!

DECREASE

In addition to providing a framework for the development of sermons, my hope for this book has been to also challenge pastors to include the work of intentionally training preachers as part of our calling. We can no longer choose to outsource the training of preachers or to hope that preachers will serendipitously develop on their own. Unless we begin to create intentional pathways to develop preachers in our local churches, many communities will find themselves without a church because of the lack of pastors to feed the flock.

The process outlined in this book would be a great place to start in your training of preachers. Each step in the DECREASE matrix would help ground developing preachers in sound practices as they begin to grow in their ability to communicate God's word.

The strategies and possible ways to train and create pathways to develop preachers are many. Check out www.thekerygmagroup.com to find additional resources I'm working on towards that end. But ultimately, a strategy won't change anything until we first change our perspective and our definition of success.

It may sound trite, but the change of heart we need is actually found in the very acronym this book is based off. As pastors we need to choose to DECREASE in order for a new generation of preachers to emerge during our lifetime and most importantly after we are gone. What do I mean by that? How do we DECREASE?

We have a choice to make as pastors, and the choice is if we will spend our lives solely building our names and our platforms or if we will use our energies towards discipling others so that the name of Jesus would be magnified above all others.

Have you stopped to consider what the impact of your life will be after you leave this earth? The Kingdom of God grows inter-generationally as one generation disciples the next. We are entrusted with the gospel and our honor is to disciple others who can pass the gospel forward in this life and after we are gone. Does your life produce the fruit of leaders that will continue the work of ministry after you fulfill your calling in this world?

Decreasing as a pastor in order to develop other preachers requires creating room for others to preach in your church. That ranges from small group settings, retreats, classes and larger gatherings such as Sunday mornings. All of this should be done with great prayer, wisdom and patience, but my argument is that it needs to get done! Put in the calendar and train people deeply in preparation for that future date. Expect progress to go slow. Don't expect a home run the first time you commit to this and don't let a foul ball become an excuse to stop developing preachers.

One practical way to do this is to take a few weeks off every year and plan for the developing preachers in your church to take on a good percentage of the preaching load, if not the majority of it. Doing this every year will communicate a few things to your church. It will instill the value of rest and self-care for you as a leader, and it will also communicate that the ministry of the word is not centered around you. By creating room for leaders who have proven faithful in your church, you are highlighting the importance of character and commitment to your church as pathway for growth in servant-leadership.

Another practical thing to do is to schedule these leaders to preach not just when you are not present, but schedule them on Sundays when you are present. Show your church that you can receive the word of God from these developing leaders and so should they. Have them preach important sessions at retreats and other settings and let the church see you receive ministry from them.

But perhaps the biggest thing to keep in mind is simply the big picture of what it will mean to DECREASE. By the time your ministry comes to a close, ideally there should be several people who you have trained and mentored that could do everything you have done, including preaching. If that is the goal, what are the things you will have to commit to in order to prepare for that day? It won't happen overnight, nor should it, but unless you commit to this overall vision and work at it every year in some intentional manner, you will miss the opportunity to pass the baton of the gospel to the next generation.

Committing to DECREASE is not easy. It will force you to face your limitations and the fact that you and I replaceable. None of us are indispensable. That's a hard pill to swallow, but a necessary one if we are going to develop preachers.

Thankfully this process is not all difficult. In fact, it's actually one of the most rewarding things you can do. There is no greater joy than to see someone grow before your eyes and experience their first steps as a preacher. It's glorious to see God use others, especially people you have helped disciple. By God's grace you will have played a significant part in their development and their success will be something you can share in with them.

Committing to DECREASE as a preacher in order to train other preachers is the best thing you can do to focus your efforts in ministry. Framing your ministry around the reality that you won't be in the saddle all of your life, and that even during your prime you should be creating room for others to develop, will focus your ministry opportunities. You and I don't have time to waste. Thus eliminating the illusion that we have more time than we actually do for direct ministry or the training of others will serve you and your church in the long run.

My prayer is that when you and I close out our ministries we will have the unique joy that only comes by choosing to die to our desire for personal greatness and focus on elevating others for the glory of God!

WORD OF CAUTION

My greatest hesitancy in writing this book has been the fear of what immature people could do with what I propose, specifically immature people who sense a call to preach. In our day and age of "self-help"and the multi-billion dollar industry around it, there is no shortage of people who are self-proclaimed experts in all sorts of things. A decent "DIY" video on YouTube could have any of us building and doing all sorts of things. The last thing I would want is for that mentality to carry over to preaching.

As much as I was motivated to level the playing field with respect to how the local church can reclaim the task of training preachers, I don't believe that just anyone can and should preach in a Sunday gathering or various other formal settings where God's people gather to learn Scripture. The reasons for my reservations or restrictive attitude are several, but I will share those most important.

To the immature this book could potentially be used as justification for aspiring preachers to simply master a process or technique and then -- presto! -- we are magically ready to preach. Nothing could be further from the truth. Hopefully our DECREASE journey has made clear that preaching is far from performance or the byproduct of steps we mechanically employ. My prayer is that as a result of reading this book your preparation to preach and the very delivery of your sermon will be more God-centered than you could have imagined possible. That being said, because I know the tendencies of my own soul, and as a pastor I'm constantly reminded that even our attempts to approach holy things can be broken themselves, I thought it would be wise to write this chapter.

Growing in the ability to prepare an actual sermon and having the maturity to stand behind a pulpit could not be further apart from each. I've met many folks over the years who could run circles around people when it came to theological knowledge, whether they were self-taught or received formal theological training. Living in New York I have met some of the most engaging communicators both within the church or, quite frankly, some of them were performing/speaking on a crowded subway platform. In prayer gatherings I've witnessed some of the most anointed, spiritually gifted people offer words of exhortation that felt as if God himself was breathing upon the room as they spoke. The number of leaders I've met over the years who have a plethora of ministry experiences, even preaching experience, would be too long a list to share. Despite having witnessed all of these things and more, the harsh reality is that all of these gifts, experiences and passions don't automatically mean that someone is called, gifted, or mature enough to preach.

Scripture teaches us in 1 Timothy 3 that we should not grant spiritual authority to a novice, lest they become filled with pride. I've seen this happen with developing preachers more times than I care to remember, and I've also personally experienced this myself. The thrill of God using us through preaching can be so immense that just one moment of preaching can change the course of a life. Not only is it thrilling, it's also deeply humbling because God glorifies himself through us despite our brokenness. Immaturity can be damaging when it leads us to think our personal holiness or individual giftedness are the reasons why God is being glorified through our preaching. The resulting pride can be quite immense and severely damaging.

The disturbing truth is that it's easy to love the act of preaching more than the God we are preaching about and more than the people we are preaching to. We can become so enamored by our own giftedness in preaching and the joy we receive from preaching that it can eclipse our hearts from seeing the glory of God. Sadly, it's not mandatory in many churches and settings for preachers to demonstrate a substantial degree of pastoral care for people before they preach, thus it's quite possible for preachers to care more about preaching at people than actually walking alongside them and loving them.

Just because we know our way around a text of Scripture and have passion, gifts, and even a grace from God to preach doesn't mean we should be behind a pulpit. This last line is hard to swallow because, in our day and age, gifted people have the world handed to them even if they don't possess the character to withstand the pressures their gifts can create on their lives. When our gifts outpace our character and when our humility lags behind our self-centered confidence, it's a recipe for disaster.

Preachers are not developed through a book or a seminar; they are forged in the crucible of failure, submitting to spiritual authority, walking vulnerably with others and deeply loving people that often don't love us back. Seminaries are useful in training preachers. But a classroom disconnected from the difficult realities of pastoring people will likely foster pride much quicker than it will prepare someone to preach effectively for the long haul.

For me, the best possible scenario would be that aspiring and developing preachers receive just as much training to be shepherds outside of the pulpit than they are receiving to pastor from behind a pulpit. In a twisted and perverted kind of way, I previously thought that pastoring people was holding me back from preaching with greater power and authority. The time it took to love people well, to correct people, to remind people again and again of what God's word says felt like it would have been time better spent in prayer and study. If only I could have devoted all that time spent pastoring to prayer and study, imagine the caliber of sermons I would preach (or so I thought)? Over the years I've come to realize this kind of thinking is deeply misguided. It took time to realize I was being prepared to preach as I was walking alongside people just as much as times of prayer and study also prepared me.

If we can't love people without a microphone in our hands, why would we think having a microphone would magically help us to do so? A microphone only magnifies our voice and carries forth the kind of people we really are. A microphone doesn't transform us as people, at least not for the better.

In the movie *The Apostle*, Robert Duvall plays the role of a deeply gifted yet troubled preacher. Throughout the movie he does amazing things for God and in the name of God. But sadly he can never outrun the shadow his jacked-up character casts on everything he touches. At a critical juncture of the movie, he enters into a small body of water in the woods somewhere and does something quite odd. He baptizes himself as an apostle. You read that right: he baptizes himself, but specifically he baptizes himself as an apostle.

The real kicker was not the baptism alone; it was the act of baptizing himself as an apostle. Part of me chuckles at this moment because, if you're going to baptize yourself as anything, you might as well swing for the fences and baptize yourself as an apostle! Right? Go for it! Sarcasm aside, this movie scene saddens me because I've seen many leaders essentially do the same thing in various ways. Many times it's done by leaving a church or ministry prematurely to pursue "their calling." Now in some cases leaving one's church may be the only way you can fulfill your calling, particularly if that church is not doctrinally sound or if the leadership culture is such that you will never receive opportunities to explore and grow in your gifts.

That being said, I have seen far too many leaders leave their church and disconnect from their mentors for reasons that seem reactionary based on immaturity. Often the decision to leave the protection of mentors is not done with much prayer and truly respectful dialogue. It's the job of pastors, teachers, evangelists, prophets and apostles along with local church elders to train people for ministry. Part of this training goes beyond intellectual content to providing a graced-filled rebuke from time to time. We can miss actual training that would move us forward in God's plan when we depart from a community that provides this sort of accountability. I hope that this book provides a conversational bridge for you and your pastor to begin to talk through what it looks like to be developed as a preacher. But I also hope it draws you closer to your spiritual mentors and your local church. May you see yourself progressing in God's calling and may you also see your participation as a vitally important link in the chain of your development.

If the principles in this book help to cut down your development time as a preacher, I pray you would use the "extra time" gained to dig deeper roots in your local church. The last thing we need are churches filled with people who have a skill or a gift without the requisite humility that comes through the crucible of true, authentic friendships. There is a great sense of urgency when it comes to the task of training preachers since less than 4% of churches are reproducing churches. Given the urgency of the hour, the only speed we should be driving is 100 miles per hour-- minimum! Churches aren't reproducing at a rate that will position the wider church to spread the Gospel and grow beyond a level of mere subsistence. We need to catch up and we need to catch up fast.

In the midst of having an intense passion to see local churches reclaiming the task of developing preachers, James 3 provides a sort of brake to that racing car. James 3:1 sends us a chilling warning as we prepare to train others to preach God's word: "Not many of you should become teachers, my fellow believers, because you know that we who teach will be judged more strictly." James tells us that we should be concerned with a desire to preach that isn't tethered to the terrifying reality that one day we will give an account for every word we speak, particularly the words we speak as preachers. The privilege of preaching is so sacred and our view of preaching should be so lofty that, though we feel called to it and find joy in it, the severity surrounding preaching should give us prayerful pause.

Based on James 3, I would encourage taking an unhurried approach to our development as preachers. By all means possess a drive to grow as a preacher and a holy determination to let God use you as a preacher. Those are good perspectives to have. But may they express themselves from a heart that lacks an unhealthy sense of hurry. One of the most surprising things to discover about our God is that he is not in a rush. The urgency of our times doesn't spur God to rush to frantic activity, employing quick remedies. God's plans are swift but they are never rushed. If God's biggest plans in history have been accomplished with this kind of divine patience, how much more is God not in a rush to develop us as preachers?

One of the best resources for your development as a preacher is found in developing a mentoring relationship with your pastor. I would encourage you to reach out to him or her and express the sense of calling that is growing in your heart towards preaching God's word. If they are like most pastors, they will be thrilled to hear this. Personally, it gives me great hope whenever someone shares they feel God calling them to pastor and preach. The church needs as many called leaders as we can get! Your pastor will be thrilled by this news. As you share it, ask them if they would mentor you into your calling and allow for that relationship to blossom over time.

But if your pastor is anything like me, the news of God stirring a call in your soul will also produce some godly concern. Pastors know firsthand the spiritual intensity that surrounds this call. As exciting as this news may be, it's kind of like receiving a report from the doctor about a condition that will alter the rest of your life. Labeling the call to preach a "condition" sounds extreme but it's really quite an accurate description. When God calls someone to preach, he is calling them to live a particular kind of life. Though all Christians are called to pray, the prayer life of preacher carries a heavy sense of responsibility. Though all Christians are called to study God's word, the life of study that a preacher must live is far from average. In order to keep the pantry of your soul full, especially if you preach regularly, it will require a discipline and focus that won't always be easy to walk out. It will require a determination and commitment that is far from average. This rhythm will be one that most people would not categorize as normal. As pastors we know these realities, so when we hear someone tell us they are called to preach, our reaction should be one of joy and simultaneous pause.

The biblical pattern for leadership development is not self-discipline and personal mastery detached from a community. Rather, the biblical pattern is leaders developing leaders in the context of close relationships. From Moses to Joshua, Elijah to Elisha, Jesus to the Apostles and Paul to Timothy, leaders have always been developed as they serve under the spiritual authority of seasoned leaders. Through the process of serving others in submission to leaders in your local church, leadership is developed over time.

My hope and prayer is that the tools offered in this book or for that matter any tools God places in our hands would equip us in skill, while arming us with sincere humility. May our gifts flourish and our callings unfold as we faithfully serve alongside our brothers and sisters, taking much needed cues and guidance from those who have gone before us.

ABOUT THE AUTHOR

Before coming Lead Pastor at Hope Astoria (www.hopeastoria.org),
Kristian served as the Director of Ministries at Resurrection Church in
Sunset Park, Brooklyn. Under the mentoring of Bishop Joseph Mattera,
Kristian grew as a minister and leader - preaching and training preachers,
leading the youth ministry for many years, discipling and counseling, and
overseeing renovation projects. Short term mission trips played a huge part
in his life, stirring an insatiable desire to see people experience the power of
God's Spirit in their lives.

He and his family live in Rockaway, NY enjoying the beach whenever they
can. Coffee is probably his best friend, and reading books make him pretty
happy. If laughing and finding humor in things were a crime, he would be
sent away for life without parole.

Kristian received his Bachelor of Arts degree in Political Science and
Economics from Brooklyn College of the City University of New York.

Made in the USA
Columbia, SC
20 April 2019